Elements: Essays on W~~riti~~

Edited by John Pfannkuc

Original essays by John Pfannkuchen an

Language updated for modern readers by

Copyright © 2019 by Elwood Learning

Elwood Learning

32 Terrace Dr

Binghamton, NY 13905

www.elwoodlearning.com

Ordering Information: Quantity sales. Special discounts are available on quantity purchases by corporations, associations, and others. For details, contact the publisher at the address above.

Orders by U.S. trade bookstores and wholesalers. Please contact Ingram Distribution at

One Ingram Blvd.,

La Vergne, TN 37086

615.793.5000

Printed in the United States of America.

Published by Elwood Learning, an imprint of Elwood Publishing.

ELEMENTS: ESSAYS ON WRITING

5) an essa[y]
a way [to] [?]
express [oneself]
and write [about]
topic from any [?]
of view [?]

The Art of the Essayist

Arthur Benson

1   There is a pleasant story of an itinerant sign-painter who in going his rounds came to a village inn whose signboard he'd had his eye on for months, and had watched with increasing hope and delight as it peeled and faded.

2   However, to his horror, he found a brand-new varnished sign. He surveyed it with disgust, and said to the inn-keeper, who stood nervously by hoping for a professional compliment, "This looks as if someone had been doing it himself."

3   That sentence holds within it the key to the whole mystery of essay-writing. An essay is a thing that someone does theirself, and the point of the essay is not the subject, for any subject will suffice, but the charm of personality. It must concern itself with something "jolly," something smelled, heard, seen, perceived, invented, thought, but the essential thing is that the writer should have formed their own impression, and that it should have taken shape in their own mind, and the charm of the essay depends upon the charm of the mind that has conceived and recorded the impression.

4   It will be seen, then, that the essay need not concern itself with anything definite; it need not have an intellectual or a philosophical or a religious or a humorous motif, but neither are these subjects are ruled out. The only thing necessary is that the thing or the thought should be vividly apprehended, enjoyed, felt to be beautiful, and expressed with a certain gusto. It need conform to no particular rules.

5   All literature answers to something in life, some habitual form of human expression. The stage imitates life, calling in the services of the eye and the ear; there is the narrative of the teller of tales or the minstrel; the song, the letter, the talk—all forms of human

expression and communication have their antitypes in literature. The essay is the reverie, the frame of mind in which a man says, in the words of the old song, "Says I to myself, says I."

6   It is generally supposed that Montaigne was the first who wrote what may technically be called essays. His pieces are partly autobiographical, partly speculative, and to a great extent ethical. But the roots of his writing lie far back in literary history. He owed a great part of his inspiration to Cicero, who treated of abstract topics in a conversational way with a romantic background, and this he owed to Plato, whose dialogues undoubtedly contain the germ of both the novel and the essay. Plato is in truth far more the forerunner of the novelist than of the philosopher. He made a background of life, he peopled his scenes with bright boys and amiable elders— oh that all scenes were so peopled!—and he discussed ethical and speculative problems of life and character with a vital rather than with a philosophical interest. Plato's dialogues would be essays but for the fact that they have a dramatic coloring, while the essence of the essay is soliloquy.

7   But in the writings of Cicero, such as the De Senectute, the dramatic interest is but slight, and the whole thing approaches far more nearly to the essay than to the novel. Cicero probably served the function both of the essayist and the preacher, and fed the needs of so-called thoughtful readers by dallying in a fashion which can justly be called twaddling, with familiar ethical problems of conduct and character. The charm of Montaigne is the charm of personality—frankness, gusto, acute observation, lively acquaintance with men and manners. He is ashamed of recording nothing that interested him; a certain discreet shamelessness must always be the characteristic of the essayist, for the essence of his art is to say what has pleased him without too prudently considering whether it is worthy of the attention of the well-informed mind.

8   I doubt if the English temperament is wholly favorable to the development of the essayist. In the first place, an Westerner likes

doing things better than thinking about them, and in his memories, he is apt to recall how a thing was done rather than why it was done. In the next place, we are naturally rather prudent and secretive; we say that a person must not wear their heart upon their sleeve, and that is just what the essayist must do. We have a horror of giving ourselves away, and we like to keep ourselves to ourselves. "The Englishman's home is his castle," says another proverb. But the essayist must not have a castle, or if one does, both the grounds and the living-rooms must be open to the inspection of the public.

9 Lord Brougham, who reveled in advertisement, used to allow his house to be seen by visitors, and the butler had orders that if a party of people came to see the house, Lord Brougham was to be informed of the fact. He used to hurry to the library and take up a book, in order that the tourists might nudge each other and say in whispers, "There is the Lord Chancellor." That is the right frame of mind for the essayist. An essayist may enjoy privacy, but they are no less delighted that people should see them enjoying it.

10 The essay has taken very various forms in England. Sir Thomas Browne, in such books as Religio Medici and Urn-Burial, wrote essays of an elaborate rhetorical style, the long fine sentences winding themselves out in delicate weft-like trails of smoke on a still air, hanging in translucent veils. Addison, in the Spectator, treated life and its problems with delicate humor, and created what was practically a new form in the essay of emotional sentiment evoked by solemn scenes and fine associations. Charles Lamb treated the homeliest stuff of life romantically, and showed how the simplest and most common experiences were rich in emotion and humor. The beauty and dignity of common life were his theme. De Quincey wrote what may be called impassioned autobiography, and brought to his task a magical control of long-drawn and musical cadences. And then we come to such a writer as Pater, who used the essay for the expression of exquisite artistic sensation.

11 These are only a few instances of the way in which the essay has

been used in English literature. But the essence is throughout the same; it is personal sensation, personal impression, evoked by something strange or beautiful or curious or interesting or amusing. Thus it has a good deal in common with the art of the lyrical poet and the writer of sonnets, but it has all the freedom of prose, its more extended range, its use of less strictly poetical effects, such as humor in particular. Humor is alien to poetical effect, because poetry demands a certain sacredness and solemnity of mood. The poet is emotional in a reverential way; he is thrilled, he loves, he worships, he sorrows; but it is all essentially grave, because he wishes to recognize the sublime and up-lifted elements of life; he wishes to free himself from all discordant, absurd, fantastic, undignified contrasts, as he would extrude laughter and chatter and comfortable ease from some stately act of ceremonial worship.

12 It is quite true that the essayist has a full right to such a mood if he chooses, and such essays as Pater's are all conceived in a sort of rapture of holiness, in a region from which all that is common and homely is carefully fenced out. But the essayist may have a larger range, and the strength of a writer like Charles Lamb is that he condescends to use the very commonest materials, and transfigures the simplest experiences with a fairy-like delicacy and a romantic glow. A poet who has more in common with the range of the essayist Robert Browning, and there are many of his poems, though not perhaps his best, where his frank amassing of grotesque detail, his desire to include rather than exclude the homelier sorts of emotion, of robust and not very humorous humor, make him an impressionist rather than a lyrist.

13 As literature develops, the distinction between poetry and prose will no doubt become harder to maintain. Coleridge said in a very fruitful maxim: "The opposite of poetry is not prose but science; the opposite of prose is not poetry but verse." That is to say poetry has as its object the kindling of emotion, and science is its opposite, because science is the dispassionate statement of fact—but prose

can equally be used as a vehicle for the kindling of emotion, and therefore may be in its essence poetical, but when it is a technical description of a certain kind of structure, its opposite is verse—language arranged in metrical and rhythmical form. We shall probably come to think that the essayist is more of a poet than the writer of epics, and that the divisions of literature will tend to be on the one hand the art of clear and logical statement, and on the other the art of emotional and imaginative expression.

14 We must remember in all this that the nomenclature of literature, the attempt to classify the forms of literary expression, is a confusing and a bewildering thing unless it is used merely for convenience. It is pedantic to say that literature must conform to established usages and types. The essence of it is that it is a large force flowing through any channel that it can, and the classification of art is a mere classification of channels. What lies behind all art is the principle of wonder and of arrested attention. It need not be only the sense of beauty; it may be the sense of fitness, of strangeness, of completeness, of effective effort.

15 The amazement of the savage at the sight of a civilized town is not the sense of beauty, it is the sense of force, of mysterious resources, of incredible products, of things unintelligibly and even magically made, and then too there is the instinct for perceiving all that is grotesque, absurd, amusing and jocose, which you can see exhibited in children at the sight of the parrot's crafty and solemn eye and his exaggerated imitation of human speech, at the unusual dress and demeanor of the clown, at the grotesque simulation by the gnarled and contorted tree of something human or reptile. And then, too, there is the strange property in human beings which makes disaster amusing, if its effects are not prejudicial to oneself; that sense which makes the waiter on the pantomime stage, who falls headlong with a tray of crockery, an object to provoke the loudest and most spontaneous mirth of which the ordinary human being is capable. The moralist who would be sympathetically shocked at

the rueful abrasions of the waiter, or mournful over the waste of human skill and endeavor involved in the breakage, would be felt by all human beings to have something priggish in his composition and to be too good, as they say, to live.

16 It is with these rudimentary and inexplicable emotions that the essayist may concern himself, even though the poet be forbidden to do so; and the appeal of the essayist to the world at large will depend upon the extent to which they experience some common emotion, sees it in all its bearings, catches the salient features of the scene, and records it in vivid and impressive speech.

17 The essayist is therefore, to a certain extent, bound to be a spectator of life; they must be like the man in Browning's fine poem "How it Strikes a Contemporary," who walked about, took note of everything, looked at the new house building, poked his stick into the mortar.

> He stood and watched the cobbler at his trade,
> The man who slices lemons into drink,
> The coffee-roaster's brazier, and the boys
> That volunteer to help him turn its winch;
> He glanced o'er books on stalls with half an eye,
> And fly-leaf ballads on the vendor's string,
> And broad-edge bold-print posters by the wall;
> He took such cognizance of men and things!
> If any beat a horse, you felt he saw;
> If any cursed a woman, he took note,
> Yet stared at nobody—they stared at him,
> And found less to their pleasure than surprise,
> He seemed to know them, and expect as much.

18 That is the essayist's material; they may choose the scene, they may select the sort of life they are interested in, whether it is the street or the countryside or the sea-beach or the picture-gallery, but once there, wherever they may be, they must devote their self to seeing and realizing and getting it all by heart. The essayist must not be too much interested in the action and conduct of life. If the essayist

is a politician, or a soldier, or an emperor, or a farmer, or a thief, and is absorbed in what they are doing, with a vital anxiety to make profit or position or influence out of it; if they hate their opponents and reward their friends; if they condemn, despise, disapprove, they at once forfeit sympathy and largeness of view. The essayist must believe with all their might in the interest of what they enjoy, to the extent at all events of believing it worth recording and representing, but he must not believe too solemnly or urgently in the importance and necessity of any one sort of business or occupation. The eminent banker, the social reformer, the forensic pleader, the fanatic, the crank, the puritan—these are not the stuff out of which the essayist is made; the essayist may have ethical preferences, but they must not indulge in moral indignation; they must be essentially tolerant, and they must discern quality rather than solidity. They must be concerned with the pageant of life, as it weaves itself with a moving tapestry of scenes and figures rather than with the aims and purposes of life. They must, in fact, be preoccupied with things as they appear, rather than with their significance or their ethical example.

19 I have little doubt in my own mind that the charm of the familiar essayist depends upon their power of giving the sense of a good-humored, gracious and reasonable personality and establishing a sort of pleasant friendship with their reader. One does not go to an essayist with a desire for information, or with an expectation of finding a clear statement of a complicated subject; that is not the mood in which one takes up a volume of essays. What one rather expects to find is a companionable treatment of that vast mass of little problems and floating ideas which are aroused and evoked by our passage through the world, our daily employment, our leisure hours, our amusements and diversions, and above all by our relations with other people—all the unexpected, inconsistent, various simple stuff of life; the essayist ought to be able to impart a certain beauty and order into it, to delineate, let us say, the vague emotions

aroused in solitude or in company by the sight of scenery, the aspect of towns, the impressions of art and books, the interplay of human qualities and characteristics, the half-formed hopes and desires and fears and joys that form so large a part of our daily thoughts.

20 The essayist ought to be able to indicate a case or a problem that is apt to occur in ordinary life and suggest the theory of it, to guess what it is that makes our moods resolute or fitful, why we act consistently or inconsistently, what it is that repels or attracts us in our dealings with other people, what our private fancies are. The good essayist is one who makes a reader say: "Well, I have often thought all those things, but I never discerned before any connection between them, nor got so far as to put them into words." And thus the essayist must have a great and far-reaching curiosity; they must be interested rather than displeased by the differences of human beings and by their varied theories. They must recognize the fact that most people's convictions are not the result of reason, but a mass of associations, traditions, things half-understood, phrases, examples, loyalties, whims. They must care more about the inconsistency of humanity than about its dignity; and they must study more what people actually do think about than what they ought to think about.

21 The essayist must not be ashamed of human weaknesses or shocked by them, and still less disgusted by them; but at the same time they must keep in mind the flashes of fine idealism, the passionate visions, the irresponsible humors, the salient peculiarities, that shoot like sun rays through the dull cloudiness of so many human minds, and make one realize that humanity is at once above itself and in itself, and that we are greater than we know, for the interest of the world to the ardent student of it is that we most of us seem to have got hold of something that is bigger than we quite know how to deal with, something remote and far off, which we have seen in a distant vision, which we cannot always remember or keep clear in our minds.

22　The supreme fact of human nature is its duality, its tendency to pull different ways, the tug-of-war between Devil and Baker which lies inside our restless brains. And the confessed aim of the essayist is to make people interested in life and in themselves and in the part they can take in life, and he does that best if he convinces men and women that life is a fine sort of a game, in which they can take a hand, and that every existence, however confined or restricted, is full of outlets and pulsing channels, and that the interest and joy of it is not confined to the politician or the millionaire, but is pretty fairly distributed, so long as one has time to attend to it, and is not preoccupied in some concrete aim or vulgar ambition.

23　Because the great secret which the true essayist whispers in our ears is that the worth of experience is not measured by what is called success, but rather resides in a fullness of life: that success tends rather to obscure and to diminish experience, and that we may miss the point of life by being too important, and that the end of it all is the degree in which we give rather than receive.

24　The poet perhaps is the man who sees the greatness of life best, because he lives most in its beauty and fineness. But my point is that the essayist is really a lesser kind of poet, working in simpler and humbler materials, more in the glow of life perhaps than in the glory of it, and not finding anything common or unclean.

25　The essayist is the opposite of the romancer, because his one and continuous aim is to keep the homely materials in view, to face actual conditions, not to fly from them. We think meanly of life if we believe that it has no sublime moments; but we think sentimentally of it if we believe that it has nothing but sublime moments. The essayist wants to hold the balance; and if he is apt to neglect the sublimities of life, it is because he is apt to think that they can take care of themselves, and that if there is the joy of adventure, the thrill of the start in the fresh air of the morning, the rapture of ardent companionship, the gladness of the arrival, yet there must be long spaces in between, when the pilgrim jogs steadily along, and seems to come no nearer to the spire on the horizon or to the shining embanked cloud land of the West. He has nothing then but his own thoughts to help him, unless he is alert to see what is happening in hedgerow and copse, and the work of the essayist is to make something rich and strange of those seemingly monotonous spaces, those lengths of level road.

26 Is, then, the essay in literature a thing which simply stands outside classification, like Argon among the elements, of which the only thing which can be predicated is that it is there? Or like Justice in Plato's Republic, a thing which the talkers set out to define, and which ends by being the one thing left in a state when the definable qualities are taken away? No, it is not that. It is rather like what is called an organ prelude, a little piece with a theme, not very strict perhaps in form, but which can be fancifully treated, modulated from, and colored at will. It is a little criticism of life at some one point clearly enough defined.

27 We may follow any mood, we may look at life in fifty different ways—the only thing we must not do is to despise or deride, out of ignorance or prejudice, the influences which affect others, because the essence of all experience is that we should perceive something which we do not begin by knowing, and learn that life has a fullness and a richness in all sorts of diverse ways which we do not at first even dream of suspecting.

28 The essayist, then, is in his particular fashion an interpreter of life, a critic of life. They do not see life as the historian, or as the philosopher, or as the poet, or as the novelist, and yet they have a touch of all these. The essayist is not concerned with discovering a theory of it all, or fitting the various parts of it into each other. They work rather on what is called the analytic method, observing, recording, interpreting, just as things strike them, and letting their fancy play over the beauty and significance; the end of it all being this: that the essayist is deeply concerned with the charm and quality of things, and desires to put it all in the clearest and gentlest

light, so that at least they may make others love life a little better, and prepare them for its infinite variety and alike for its joyful and mournful surprises.

On Inspiration

John Pfannkuchen

1   As a person who never knows what to do, or when to do it, I am always envious of the passionate and resolute poet, artist, film maker, or musician, struck by a bolt of inspiration, toiling away into the little hours, with sweat working down their brow, as their fingers cramp and their back twists, sacrificing joyfully their bodies to bring to the world some vision. It seems that rather the vision is the boss of the artist, is in control of the artist, and doing all the work, rather than the artist—yet it's the artist that gets all the credit!

2   That looks easy, or at least fun, I say to myself, taking credit for a genius that is not mine. What's wrong with me, that I'd rather lie on the couch very still, and watch my feet, like little headstones rising from the cushion? I wonder to myself where can inspiration be got? Do they sell it at the gas station, in little bottles beside the card machine, along with five hour energy drinks and sticks of bubblegum? I've tried everything on that counter individually and in horrible combination. The result was jittery steps, a sore jaw, and an overwhelming feeling of spearmint. But alas, no inspiration.

3   Sometimes I will sit down at a cafe and think to myself, "Now is the time to be productive. Now is the time to write, or draw, or to do...something! Inspiration...Come to me!"

4   And then when nothing happens, my solution is to berate myself. "Listen, self," I say, "Why are you so lazy? What's wrong with you?" I imagine the accomplished writers in their mid 40s, the young prodigy, the towering legends, all my heroes, Shakespeare, for crying out loud, all of their eyes glowing in the darkness, hovering above me, pressing down on me. Soon I can't breathe properly, it feels stuffy, warm, my inability to move feels like a sin, and so I

stand and move to my desk, slowly, and shamefully. Because, you see dear reader, the guilt of the writer is two-fold, you feel guilty for not writing, but when you try to write, you feel guilty for not writing well enough.

5 So I finally lift a pen, heavy as iron chains, and hoist it over a piece of parchment, and heaving it left and right, make some scant forms resembling symbols, which may or may not convey sounds that, when combined create words in our language—every single one of those phantoms sneer, laugh, jeer, heckle and shout; a din of frothing geniuses and prodigies and heroes, cruel and contemptuous, and well—not very friendly.

6 One has to have the gall to sit at that desk and endure it. One has to have resilience. How this strength comes about I do not know. But I will tell you a secret, though it may seem obvious once I reveal it. The secret is this: once you begin writing, and rewriting, and rearranging, and reading, and rereading, and editing, I often find that the horrible din subsides, dies down, fades into the background. It's never totally gone, at least not for long—but it becomes a part of the white noise that is the writing process. I have learned to drown the evil out with the sounds of my own toil. "Never mind the people who are so much better at this than I," I say to myself, "I have work to do."

7 But it's just getting started that is so hard! In fact the harder I try to start, the less inspired I feel. But never mind that, I pick up my pen and I begin. My philosophy is that, if I am to be a bad writer, then so be it. I shall write badly—but productively. That is, I will get all the bad, stupid, cliché, hackneyed words, thoughts and ideas onto the page, quickly and with as little fanfare as possible, so that once it's done and out of me, hopefully I can pan some gold from the silt. I start a list. I write down all of the obvious stuff. All the droll and boring and useless stuff. Everything—everything I can think of. I get it onto the page. And once I've exhausted these things I keep going, finding more and more, pushing myself, until eventu-

ally I hit oil, or scratch through the skin and draw blood—here is something truly stupid, I think, but hey—something no one has thought of. It's stupid, but it's not cliché, or obvious, or hackneyed. It's original stupidity, and that's something.

8 That's how I discovered the humble list. I find lists easy to write, and it takes less time to make changes to a list than to a finished draft. Once I really get going, and start branching out into different kinds of lists, they become extensions of my thoughts and memories. It seems the more I use lists to remember and brainstorm, the longer my lists become, and the better I get at using them.

9 I list all my first impressions. I don't impose any kind of order or priority of any kind on the list, because I know the moment I start forcing myself to organize the whole thing this art will feel like work, and then I'll end up back on the couch. I tell myself that tomorrow, when my muse finally visits me, I can jumble everything around and reorder it without consequence. But for now I'll have to do without a muse, or a vision, or inspiration.

10 The next day I embellish my lists without removing anything. And if I should notice or think of something new, or make a connection, they are added to the list. Only when I feel I have written the world's most complete list do I begin forming whole sentences—comprised of thoughts, observations and impressions. I especially like to dwell on the combination of thoughts which are closely related. With these lists I can then plan more research for future days, and from that research I may eventually spin more lists.

On the Illness of My Muse

Hilaire Belloc

1   The other day I noticed that my Muse, who had long been ailing, silent and morose, was showing signs of actual illness.

2   Now, though it is by no means one of my habits to coddle the dogs, cats and other familiars of my household, yet my Muse had so pitiful an appearance that I determined to send for the doctor, but not before I had seen her to bed with a hot bottle, a good supper, and such other comforts as the Muses are accustomed to value. All that could be done for the poor girl was done thoroughly; a fine fire was lit in her bedroom, and a great number of newspapers such as she is given to reading for her recreation were bought at a neighboring shop. When she had drunk her wine and read in their entirety the Daily Telegraph, the Morning Post, the Standard, the Daily Mail, the Daily Express, the Times, the Daily News, and even the Advertiser, I was glad to see her sink into a profound slumber.

3   I will confess that the jealousy which is easily aroused among servants when one of their number is treated with any special courtesy gave me some concern, and I was at the pains of explaining to the household not only the grave indisposition from which the Muse suffered, but also the obligation I was under to her on account of her virtues: which were, her long and faithful service, her willingness, and the excess of work which she had recently been compelled to perform. Her fellow-servants, to my astonishment and pleasure, entered at once into the spirit of my apology: the maid offered to sit up with her all night, or at least until the trained nurse should arrive, and the groom of the chambers, with a good will that I confess was truly surprising in one of his proud nature, volunteered to go himself and order straw for the street from a neighboring stable.

4   The cause of this affection which the Muse had aroused in the whole household I subsequently discovered to lie in her own amiable and unselfish temper. She had upon two occasions inspired the knife-boy to verses which had subsequently appeared in the Spectator, and with weekly regularity she would lend her aid to the cook in the composition of those technical reviews by which she increased her ample wages.

5   The Muse had slept for a full six hours when the doctor arrived—a specialist in these matters and one who has before now been called in (I am proud to say) by such great persons as Mr. Hichens, Mr. Churchill, and Mr. Roosevelt when their Muses have been out of sorts. Indeed, he is that doctor who operated for aphasia upon the Muse of the late Mr. Rossetti just before his demise. His fees are high, but I was willing enough to pay, and certainly would never have consented—as have, I regret to say, so many of my unworthy contemporaries—to employ a veterinary surgeon upon such an occasion.

6   The great specialist approached with a determined air the couch where the patient lay, awoke her according to the ancient formula, and proceeded to question her about her symptoms. He soon discovered their gravity, and I could see by his manner that he was anxious to an extreme. The Muse had grown so weak as to be unable to dictate even a little blank verse, and the indisposition had so far affected her mind that she had no memory of Parnassus, but deliriously maintained that she had been born in the home counties—nay, in the neighborhood of Uxbridge. Her every phrase was a deplorable commonplace, and, on the physician applying a stethoscope and begging her to attempt some verse, she could give us nothing better than a sonnet upon the expansion of the Empire. Her weakness was such that she could do no more than awake, and that feebly, while she professed herself totally unable to arise, to expand, to soar, to haunt, or to perform any of those exercises which are proper to her profession.

7   When his examination was concluded the doctor took me aside and asked me upon what letters the patient had recently fed. I told him upon the daily Press, some of the reviews, the telegrams from the latest seat of war, and occasionally a debate in Parliament. At this he shook his head and asked whether too much had not recently been asked of her. I admitted that she had done a very considerable amount of work for so young a Muse in the past year, though its quality was doubtful, and I hastened to add that I was the less to blame as she had wasted not a little of her powers upon others without asking my leave, notably upon the knife-boy and the cook.

8   The doctor was then good enough to write out a prescription in Latin and to add such general recommendations as are commonly of more value than physic. She was to keep her bed, to be allowed no modern literature of any kind, unless Milton and Swift may be admitted as moderns, and even these authors and their predecessors were to be admitted in very sparing quantities. If any signs of inversion, archaism[1], or neologistic[2] tendencies appeared he was to be summoned at once, but of these (he added) he had little fear. He did not doubt that in a few weeks we should have her up and about again, but he warned me against letting her begin work too soon.

9   "I would not," he said, "permit her to undertake any effort until she can inspire within one day of twelve hours at least eighteen quatrains, and those lucid, grammatical, and moving. As for single lines, tags, fine phrases, and the rest, they are no sign whatever of returning health, if anything of the contrary."

10   He also begged that she might not be allowed any Greek or Latin for ten days, but I reassured him upon the matter by telling him that she was totally unacquainted with those languages—at which he expressed some pleasure but even more astonishment.

---

1 The retention or imitation of what is old or obsolete; the employment in language, art, etc., of the characteristics of an earlier period; archaic style.

2 Characterizing or about new words or forms; regarding an innovation in language.

11 At last he told me that he was compelled to be gone; the season had been very hard, nor had he known so general a breakdown among the Muses of his various clients.

12 I thought it polite as I took him to the door to ask after some of his more distinguished patients; he was glad to say that the Archbishop of Armagh's was very vigorous indeed, in spite of the age of her illustrious master. He had rarely known a more inventive or courageous female, but when, as I handed him into his carriage, I asked after that of Mr. Kipling, his face became suddenly grave, and he asked me, "Have you not heard?"

13 "No," said I, but I had a fatal presentiment of what was to follow, and indeed I was almost prepared for it when he answered in solemn tones:

14 "She is dead."

Free Write

John Pfannkuchen

1   When I find myself writing something complex, that has a lot of moving parts, I tend to feel torn between one part of an essay and another, or one stage of composition and a later stage. I have found that my mind spends a surprising amount of time planning, predicting, and imagining--sometimes without my noticing, until I realize I've been working for hours and have nothing to show for it.

2   I have tried thinking more, drawing detailed outlines, staring at walls, and pounding desks to be of little use. What should I do when my thinking gets in the way of writing? Then I wonder: what if it's this awareness of myself, and the writing process, that stops me in my tracks? So I've decided that in my case thinking and worrying too much may be the problem. If this is truly my problem, then the most confounding, and yet most obvious fact, about thinking too much is that the one thing that cannot solve it is more thinking.

3   So what's the obvious answer? Well, to think less, I suppose. But how am I supposed to write without thinking? So here's a technique that I draw on nowadays, that I learned in creative writing classes in my college days, that has stuck with me ever since. I find it works wonders for turning the brain off and just accomplishing a draft quickly.

4   Instead of just thinking about my topic, I give myself some sort of object to focus on. It can be a photograph, or place to write about from my thoughts, recordings or observations.

5   Then I put my pen to the paper and start just writing any old thing that comes to mind about the object. Once my pen is moving, I must keep it moving at all costs; recording everything—and

anything. Even if it's nonsense, circular, or just observations regarding the room. I do not stop to read what I have written. I do not erase anything. I do not correct mistakes of grammar or spelling. I remind myself that revision can be done after the session is over. When I write in this manner I do nothing but transfer words from thin air to the page, banishing my mind from the process.

6   Of course it goes without saying that working in a quiet environment (or one filled with white noise), with no video games, powered smart phones, friends, relatives, cats, dogs, parakeets, or nosy strangers is a must. I'll go to my room, or find a spot in a cafe and if a friendly person should look about ready to say something to me, or ask me what I'm up to, I scowl at them—trying to look very serious and busy. Don't bother me I project, I need to get this done!

7   For the aspiring free writer I would say that the greatest asset of free writing is its simplicity. One must empty their mind, and even though an essayist may be distracted at first, she should continue writing until all distractions have melted away, then continue writing for as long as she can. She will know when it is time to rest. Her timer will ring, her hand will start to cramp. She can take a minute and rest, get up and walk around, then come back and look at what's been written. Then the essayist must ask: is there no more I can add? Some detail I missed?

8   After, if I feel as though I have written in a shallow manner, I look back at the writing. It's not unusual that I am left with a sense of dread about the quality of the writing this technique produces, yet it usually reads better than I think it would. I think this dread are the phantoms in my head lashing out at me for sending them to the corner while I got work done, like petulant children. But if the work I produce truly is as bad as I suspect, I simply ask myself if there's anything I can do with the ideas that are there.

9   Here's something else I do: I use lists to guide my free writing. What I'll do is create a loose outline out of lists, and then free write

between the points of the list. I use each point as a free writing prompt, focusing like a laser on just that small part of the work. If my free writing causes me to ask new questions, then I do additional research! If this writing and additional research changes everything about my argument, then I update my lists as I work.

10 Here's another form of writing that I do. It's called free association. What I do is look at points in my lists, and choose a word there. What is the first thing I imagine? Whatever it is, I write that thing down, and describe it using my imagination.

11 Consider this: what do you see when you read the word "storm"? Do you picture a cloud? A flash of lightning? Perhaps a flooded sewer drain, or a tree bent over in the wind? Whatever you imagine, that is what you associated first with the word "storm." Perhaps you're a visual person, and imagined more than one thing. Perhaps you imagined a whole scene. Write what you saw down as quickly as you can. Everything, leaving nothing out. Did you hear rolling thunder? Did you feel the cold rain falling upon your arms? Did you breathe the dust, swept in a wind from the spring thaw? Whatever you imagined, begin there.

12 Now either go back to the last word you free wrote about, or choose another word. Repeat the entire process over again. This is called "looping" by some, but "writing associatively" by others. Writing by association is effective because as we write we encode our experiences with language. Language is all interconnected within our culture, just like our memories and thoughts.

13 I like to think that our imaginations are a small part of a bigger network. This network is shared with everyone who speaks the same language. What makes this interesting is that we all have different experiences, and the experiences we do share are never encoded in exactly the same way. Which is why when I read about familiar experiences they seem new and interesting. I've decided that that's how reading can build empathy, and allow us to "broaden" our minds. We're just gaining access to more and more of the

big net that is our shared experience.

14 So regardless of how one associates the word "storm." Someone out there will be touched, surprised, or bewildered by the associations. I believe that's a good thing.

Of the Motion of Thoughts in Speaking and Writing

Margaret Cavendish

1   Those that have very quick thoughts speak more often and easier than they write, because when speaking they are not tied to any style or number. Besides, in speaking, thoughts lie loose and careless, but in writing they are gathered up, and are like water in a cup whose mouth is held downward, because every drop trying to get out first stops the passage, or rather these thoughts are like everyday people in an uproar that run without order, and cannot get out. When slow and strong thoughts come well-armed and in good order, they discharge with courage, and go off with honour.

2   Of study: the reason why study seems difficult at first, and easier and clearer afterward, is, that the imagination has not beaten out a pathway of understanding in the head; and when it has, the thoughts run even and well without the pains of deep study: because when the way is made, they do not need to search long to find what they are looking for, because the brakes and rubbish of ignorance, that obstruct our thoughts, are trodden into firm and hard ground on the way to knowledge.

3   Of writers: Most modern writers only dress up old authors in new clothes, and though they dress them differently, the person is the same. But some do disguise these old authors so much, that an untrained eye cannot see it, and mistake the author through the alteration of the habit. A history and a romancy is more delightful in general than fiction, because women and fools enjoy stories; but no one but intellectuals enjoy one another.

4   Of translators: it is not enough for translators to be educated in several languages. There must be a sympathy between the genius of

the author and the translator, which every age does not produce: for most commonly a great genius is not matched in every age. Ovid's genius was matched by Sands, and Dabartos was matched by Sylvester; for, though his work was translated, it was not translated well. It is true, that though the copy of a picture is not so well as the original; the good copies are so similar to real life that no one but a curious and skillful observor can see the difference. So a good translator will write so like the original author, that no one but the most educated, and only with great study and great observation, will see the mistakes.

On the Pleasure of Taking Up One's Pen

Hilaire Belloc

1 Among the sadder and smaller pleasures of this world I count this pleasure: the pleasure of taking up one's pen.

2 It has been said by very many people that there is a tangible pleasure in the mere act of writing: in choosing and arranging words. It has been denied by many. It is affirmed and denied in the life of Doctor Johnson, and for my part I would say that it is very true in some rare moods and wholly false in most others. However, of writing and the pleasure in it I am not writing here (with pleasure), but of the pleasure of taking up one's pen, which is quite another matter.

3 Note what the action means. You are alone. Even if the room is crowded (as was the smoking-room in the G.W.R. Hotel, at Paddington, only the other day, when I wrote my "Statistical Abstract of Christendom"), even if the room is crowded, you must have made yourself alone to be able to write at all. You must have built up some kind of wall and isolated your mind. You are alone, then; and that is the beginning.

4 If you consider at what pains men are to be alone: how they climb mountains, enter prisons, profess monastic vows, put on eccentric daily habits, and seclude themselves in the garrets of a great town, you will see that this moment of taking up the pen is not least happy in the fact that then, by a mere association of ideas, the writer is alone.

5 So much for that. Now not only are you alone, but you are going to "create".

6 When people say "create" they flatter themselves. No man can create

anything. I knew a man once who drew a horse on a bit of paper to amuse the company and covered it all over with many parallel streaks as he drew. When he had done this, an aged priest (present upon that occasion) said, "You are pleased to draw a zebra." When the priest said this the man began to curse and to swear, and to protest that he had never seen or heard of a zebra. He said it was all done out of his own head, and he called heaven to witness, and his patron saint (for he was of the Old English Territorial Catholic Families—his patron saint was Aethelstan), and the salvation of his immortal soul he also staked, that he was as innocent of zebras as the babe unborn. But there! He persuaded no one, and the priest scored. It was most evident that the Territorial was crammed full of zebraical knowledge.

7   All this, then, is a digression, and it must be admitted that there is no such thing as a man's "creating". But anyhow, when you take up your pen you do something devilish pleasing: there is a prospect before you. You are going to develop a germ: I don't know what it is, and I promise you I won't call it creation—but possibly a god is creating through you, and at least you are making believe at creation. Anyhow, it is a sense of mastery and of origin, and you know that when you have done, something will be added to the world, and little destroyed. For what will you have destroyed or wasted? A certain amount of white paper at a farthing a square yard (and I'm not convinced the paper is less pleasant diversified and variegated[1] with black wriggles)—a certain amount of ink meant to be spread and dried: made for no other purpose. A certain infin-itesimal amount of quill—torn from the silly goose for no purpose whatsoever but to minister to the high needs of Man.

8   Here you cry "Affectation! Affectation! How do I know that the fellow writes with a quill? A most unlikely habit!" To that I answer you are right. Less assertion, please, and more humility. I will tell you frankly with what I am writing. I am writing with a Water-

1   Marked with patches or spots of different colours; varied in colour; of diverse or various colours; many-coloured, vari-coloured.

man's Ideal Fountain Pen. The nib is of pure gold, as was the throne of Charlemagne, in the "Song of Roland." That throne (I need hardly tell you) was borne into Spain across the cold and awful passes of the Pyrenees by no less than a hundred and twenty mules, and all the Western world adored it, and trembled before it when it was set up at every halt under pine trees, on the upland grasses. For he sat upon it, dreadful and commanding: there weighed upon him two centuries of age; his brows were level with justice and experience, and his beard was so tangled and full, that he was called "bramble-bearded Charlemagne." You have read how, when he stretched out his hand at evening, the sun stood still till he had found the body of Roland? No? You must read about these things.

9 Well then, the pen is of pure gold, a pen that runs straight away like a willing horse, or a jolly little ship; indeed, it is a pen so excellent that it reminds me of my subject: the pleasure of taking up one's pen.

10 God bless you, pen! When I was a boy, and they told me work was honorable, useful, cleanly, sanitary, wholesome, and necessary to the mind of man, I paid no more attention to them than if they had told me that public men were usually honest, or that pigs could fly. It seemed to me that they were merely saying silly things they had been told to say. Nor do I doubt to this day that those who told me these things at school were but preaching a dull and careless round. But now I know that the things they told me were true. God bless you, pen of work, pen of drudgery, pen of letters, pen of posings, pen rabid, pen ridiculous, pen glorified. Pray, little pen, be worthy of the love I bear you, and consider how noble I shall make you some day, when you shall live in a glass case with a crowd of tourists round you every day from 10 to 4; pen of justice, pen of the saeva indignatio, pen of majesty and of light. I will write with you some day a considerable poem; it is a compact between you and me. If I cannot make one of my own, then I will write out some other man's; but you, pen, come what may, shall write out a

good poem before you die, if it is only the Allegro.

11 The pleasure of taking up one's pen has also this, peculiar among all pleasures, that you have the freedom to lay it down when you will. Not so with love. Not so with victory. Not so with glory.

12 Had I begun the other way round, I would have called this Work, "The Pleasure of laying down one's Pen." But I began it where I began it, and I am going on to end it just where it is going to end.

13 What other occupation, avocation, dissertation, or intellectual recreation can you cease at will? Not bridge—you go on playing to win. Not public speaking—they ring a bell. Not mere converse—you have to answer everything the other insufficient person says. Not life, for it is wrong to kill one's self; and as for the natural end of living, that does not come by one's choice; on the contrary, it is the most capricious of all accidents.

14 But the pen you lay down when you will. At any moment: without remorse, without anxiety, without dishonor, you are free to do this dignified and final thing (I am just going to do it)… You lay it down.

Observation Through a Lens

John Pfannkuchen

1   Sometimes I like to imagine having a pair of glasses with dozens of different colored lenses. Each pair of lenses, when popped into the frame, "filter out" objects, people, or actions so that I can only see certain types of things.

2   I'll pop on a pair of "historical lenses," and look at the buildings around, removing everything newer than 1835. What is left? Some old rail road tracks, main street and front street and River Row, and a few buildings that today are crumbling but were brand new almost 200 years ago. I take some notes.

3   Then I'll pop in my aesthetic lenses, and find out what are the main colors, are the shapes sharp, dull, liquid, flowing, or harsh? Are the patterns geometric, or calico? What's the atmosphere? What's the mood? Why? Then I make a list.

4   Then I begin to wonder about nature, and put on my ecosystem lens, and observe the weather, the season, the geography—atop a mountain, or at the foot of an ocean? This leads me to my economic lenses, dealing with currency and consumers—the machinations and movements of mankind, as a means of production and the like, of buying and selling. When everything is stripped away human interaction becomes a series of transactions, and I can see the transfer of wealth and power. Reminded of power, I reach for my sociological lenses, and wonder how do these people relate to each other? Are some rich, or some poor? Husband or wife? Politicians or outcasts?

5   Then I take a step back, and think about the hidden systems of meaning—the symbols, metaphor and analogy—of parallels and comparisons, I watch for the words of power, logos, hand signs, gestures, movements of eye and mouth that "stand in" for other

things, like place-holders. When I see something mysterious I wonder: what else could this mean?

6 By using my lenses I am discovering my topic by figuring out what interests me. In the last task, what lens did I write the most about? This is an indicator to me of what I'll probably be writing about. I find it's always best to follow my interests and curiosity, instead of what may seem the easiest topic. When I am truly interested the essay writes itself. But writing about something I think will be easier? Easier but boring topics typically result in writing that strikes me as dull. As my enthusiasm falls ill, and my muse is nowhere to be found, I wonder if the reader might feel the same.

Ideas

Arthur Benson

1 There are certain great ideas which, if we have any intelligence and thoughtfulness at all, we cannot help coming across the track of, just as when we walk far into the deep country, in the time of the blossoming of flowers, we step for a moment into a waft of fragrance, cast upon the air from orchard or thicket or scented field of bloom.

2 These ideas are very various in quality; some of them deliciously haunting and transporting, some grave and solemn, some painfully sad and strong. Some of them seem to hint at unseen beauty and joy, some have to do with problems of conduct and duty, some with the relation in which we wish to stand or are forced to stand with other human beings; some are questionings born of grief and pain, what the meaning of sorrow is, whether pain has a further intention, whether the spirit survives the life which is all that we can remember of existence; but the strange thing about all these ideas is that we find them suddenly in the mind and soul; we do not seem to invent them, though we cannot trace them; and even if we find them in books that we read or words that we hear, they do not seem wholly new to us; we recognize them as things that we have dimly felt and perceived, and the reason why they often have so mysterious an effect upon us is that they seem to take us outside of ourselves, further back than we can recollect, beyond the faint horizon, into something as wide and great as the illimitable sea or the depths of sunset sky.

3 Some of these ideas have to do with the constitution of society, the combined and artificial peace in which human beings live, and then they are political ideas; or they deal with such things as numbers, curves, classes of animals and plants, the soil of the earth, the changes of the seasons, the laws of weight and mass, and then

they are scientific ideas; some have to do with right and wrong conduct, actions and qualities, and then they are religious or ethical ideas. But there is a class of thoughts which belong precisely to none of these things, but which are concerned with the perception of beauty, in forms and colors, musical sounds, human faces and limbs, words majestic or sweet; and this sense of beauty may go further, and may be discerned in qualities, regarded not from the point of view of their rightness and justice, but according as they are fine and noble, evoking our admiration and our desire; and these are poetical ideas.

4   It is not of course possible exactly to classify ideas, because there is a great overlapping of them and a wide interchange. The thought of the slow progress of man from something rude and beast like, the statement of the astronomer about the swarms of worlds swimming in space, may awaken the sense of poetry which is in its essence the sense of wonder. I shall not attempt in these few pages to limit and define the sense of poetry. I shall merely attempt to describe the kind of effect it has or may have in life, what our relation is or may be to it, what claim it may be said to have upon us, whether we can practice it, and whether we ought to do so.

On Paragraphs

John Pfannkuchen

5 Imagine a wall, like those of a prison, or of a skyscraper, or standing at the base of the Hoover Dam (with the water drained, of course). Whenever I stand next to a very large wall, I am made to feel all the more small, and I imagine horrible things, like the wall collapsing upon me. This is the same feeling I get from looking at a page of text that has no paragraphs. It feels imposing, and I have a hard time getting myself to begin. I think humans have a hard time reading walls of text. For me, it is easy for my eyes to become lost among the text. Aside from its imposing nature, the wall of text gives me no sense of meaning, no context. It is the whiteness of the whale; the blackness of night—it is bleak and meaningless and fills me with dread. On the other than, shorter paragraphs comfort me with the notion that there is an end and a beginning, and armed with a sense of what's in store, I begin merrily, knowing feeling some sense of progress and accomplishment with the completion of each paragraph.

6 A divided piece of writing, in which the author has a natural feel for when to hit the Enter (Return) key, flows like a familiar song, giving the work a sense of rhythm, as do the words and sentences that make them up.

7 Even better are paragraphs that are topical in nature, that is, broken up into the smallest possible subtopics. To quote William Strunk, the Cornell professor who authored the original Elements of Style:

8 "A subject requires subdivision into topics, each of which should be made the subject of a paragraph. The object of treating each topic in a paragraph by itself is, of course, to aid the reader. The beginning of each paragraph is a signal to him that a new step in the development of the subject has been reached."

9 And as a writer myself, I find that crafting paragraphs, at first, isn't so hard. Paragraphing can be done along the way, especially if the essayist is experienced and has a firm grasp of what they are saying, or if they're following an outline. If, however, the writer has little sense of what the finished product will look like, they can always reset the paragraphs upon revision, rereading and deciding what stays, what goes, and how to organize the rest.

10 Using well defined, topical paragraphs is more than just an aid for readers, however. As an essayist it allows me to do magical things within the revision process, especially if I am working on a computer: I can merely pick up a subtopic in the form of a paragraph and move it around, without making a mess of things, assuming the paragraphs are self contained and somewhat modular in nature.

11 However, a question I often struggle with is, after the paragraphs are in the most effective order, whether to add some sort of transition between them, or leave them in a minimalist fashion, asking the reader to make the leap on their own...?

An Essay On Essays

Katharine Fullerton Gerould

1   Some of the rhetoric books my generation used in college went back to Aristotle for many of their definitions. "Rhetoric," he says, "may be defined as a faculty of discovering all the possible means of persuasion in any subject." Persuasion, indeed, is the purpose of the essay more so than of fiction or poetry, since the essay deals always with an idea. No essay is truly an essay, regardless of how unfocused or informal it is, unless it states a proposition for the reader to accept. Though it be only the defense of a mood, subject and predicate are the bare bones of any essay. It may be of a complex nature (like many of Emerson's) stating several propositions; but unless it states at least one proposition, it is not an essay. It may be a dream or a poem, but I repeat, it is not an essay.

2   Let us neglect the old rhetorical differences between exposition [story narrative] and argument. To sort all essays into those two types of writing would be more troublesome a task than any task a wicked stepmother gave to her stepdaughter in a fairy-tale. We can no more do it without the help of magic than could the poor princess. When is an essay argument, and when is it exposition— who knows?

3   Regardless, in so far as the essay attempts to persuade, it partakes of the nature of argument. Yet who would call Lamb's "Dream Children" an argument? Or who shall say it is not an essay? It contains a proposition, if you will only look for it; yet to associate Lamb's persuading process with the forum would be preposterous. All writing presupposes an audience (which some of our younger writers seem to forget) but formal argument presupposes opponents, and I cannot find the faintest scent of an enemy at hand in "Dream Children."

4   Let us now forget the rhetoricians, and use our own words (our

common sense too, if we have any). Let us say, first, that the purpose of the essay is persuasion; and that the essay states a proposition. Indeed, we need to be as rigorously simple as that, if we are going to consider briefly a type that is supposed to include Bacon's "Of Truth," De Quincey's "Murder as a Fine Art," Lamb's "In Praise of Chimney Sweeps," Hazlitt's "On Going a Journey," Irving's "Bachelors," Hunt's "Getting up on Cold Mornings," Poe's "The Poetic Principle," Emerson's "Self-Reliance," Arnold's "Function of Criticism," Stevenson's "Penny Plain and Twopence Colored," Paul Elmer More's "The Demon of the Absolute," Chesterton's "On Leisure," Max Beerbohm's "No. 2. The Pines," Stephen Leacock's "People We Know," and James Truslow Adams' "The Mucker Pose."

5   The foregoing list, in itself, confesses our main difficulty in delimiting the essay. The most popular kind of essay, perhaps, is that known as "familiar." When people deplore the passing of the essay from the pages of our magazines, it is usually this that they are regretting. They are thinking wistfully of pieces of prose like Lamb's "Sarah Battle on Whist," Leigh Hunt's "The Old Gentleman," Stevenson's "El Dorado," Max Beerbohm's "Mobled King." They mean the essay that is largely descriptive, more or less sentimental or humorous, in which it is sometimes difficult to find a stated proposition. This kind of prose has not been very popular since [World War I], and I for one, am not regretting it. It will come back—as long as the ghost of Montaigne is permitted to revisit the glimpses of the moon. But the familiar-essay-which-is-hardly-an-essay can be spared for a few years if necessary, since it demands literary gifts of a very high order, and the authors mentioned have at present no competitors in this field. If the bones of the essay are to be weak, the flesh must be exceeding fair and firm.

6   Are we to admit, at all, that "Sarah Battle" and "The Old Gentleman," and "El Dorado" and "Mobled King" are essays? Do they state a proposition to which they attempt to persuade us? Well, we can twist them to a proposition, if we are very keen on our defini-

tion—though I think most of us would admit that they are chiefly descriptive and that they are only gently directed to the creation of opinion. Must we then deny that they are essays? No, I think they are essays, though it is obvious that the familiar essayist goes about his business far otherwise than Arnold or Emerson or Macaulay. They attempt to sharpen our perceptions rather than convince us of a statement; win our sympathy rather than our suffrage. Their proposition is less important to them than their mood. If put to it, we can sift a proposition out of each one of these—and they were especially chosen because they put our definition on its defense. Lamb states, if you like, that to abide by the rigor of the game is in its way an admirable thing; Leigh Hunt states, if you like, that growing old is a melancholy business; Stevenson states that it is better to travel hopefully than to arrive; Max Beerbohm states that no man is worthy to be reproduced as a statue. But the author's proposition, in such essays, is not our main interest. This brings us to another consideration which may clarify the matter.

7   Though an essay must state a proposition, there are other requirements to be fulfilled. The bones of subject and predicate must be clothed in a certain way. The basis of the essay is meditation, and it must in a measure admit the reader to the meditative process. (This procedure is frankly hinted in all those titles that used to begin with "Of" or "On": "Of Truth," "Of Riches," "On the Graces and Anxieties of Pig-Driving," "On the Knocking at the Gate in 'Macbeth'," "On the Enjoyment of Unpleasant Places"). An essay, to some extent, thinks aloud; though not in the loose and pointless way to which the "stream of consciousness" addicts have accustomed us. The author must have made up his mind—otherwise, where is his proposition? But the essay, I think, should show how and why they made up their mind as they did; should engagingly rehearse the steps by which they came to their conclusions. ("Francis of Verulam reasoned thus with himself.") Meditation; but an oriented and fruitful meditation.

8   This is the most intimate of forms, because it permits you to see a mind at work. On the quality and temper of that mind depends the goodness of the production. Now, if the essay is essentially meditative, it cannot be polemical. No one, I think, would call Cicero's first oration against Catiline an essay; or Burke's Speech on the Conciliation of America; hardly more could we call Swift's "Modest Proposal" a true essay. The author must have made up his mind, but when they have made it up with a vengeance, they will not produce an essay. Because the process is meditative, the manner should be courteous; they should always, by implication, admit that there are good people who may not agree with them; their irony should never turn to the sardonic. Reasonableness, urbanity (as Matthew Arnold would have said) are prerequisites for a form whose temper is meditative rather than polemical.

9   We have said that this is the most intimate of forms. Not only for technical reasons, though obviously the essayist is less sharply controlled by his structure than the dramatist or the sonneteer or even the novelist. It is the most intimate because it is the most subjective. When people talk of "creative" and "critical" writing— dividing all literature thus—they always call the essay critical. In spite of Oscar Wilde, to call it critical is probably correct; for creation implies objectivity. The created thing, though the author have torn its raw substance from his very vitals, ends by being separate from its creator. The essay, however, is incurably subjective.

10 A lot of criticism is more delightful than the prose or verse that is being criticized. It is nonetheless criticism. Wilde is to some extent right when he says that criticism is the only civilized form of autobiography; but he is not so right when he says that the highest criticism is more creative than creation. All Bacon's essays together but build up a portrait of Bacon reasoning with himself; and what is the substance of the Essays of Elia, but Elia? "Subjective" is the word, however, rather than "creative."

11 It is this subjectivity that has confused many minds. It is subjec-

tivity run wild that has tempted many people to believe that the familiar essay alone is the essay; which would make some people contend that an essay does not necessarily state a proposition. But we are talking of the essay itself; not of those bits of whimsical prose which are to the true essay what expanded anecdote is to the short story.

12 The essay, then, having persuasion for its object, states a proposition; its method is meditation; it is subjective rather than objective, critical rather than creative. It can never be a mere marshaling of facts; for it struggles, in one way or another, for truth; and truth is something one arrives at by the help of facts, not the facts themselves. Meditating on facts may bring one to truth; facts alone will not. Nor can there be an essay without a point of view and a personality. A geometrical proposition cannot be an essay, since, though it arranges facts in a certain pattern, there is involved no personal meditative process, conditioned by the individuality of the author. A geometrical proposition is not subjective. One is even tempted to say that its tone is not urbane!

13 Perhaps—with the essay thus defined—we shall understand without effort why it is being so little written at present. The whole world is living more or less in a state of war; and a state of war produces any literary form more easily than the essay. It is not hard to see why. People in a state of war, whether the war be military or economic, express themselves polemically. A wise man said to me, many years ago, that, in his opinion, the worst by-product of the World War was propaganda. Many times, in the course of the years, I have had occasion to recall that statement. There are perhaps times and places where propaganda is justified—it is not for me to say. But I think we should all agree that the increasing habit of using the technique of propaganda is corrupting the human mind in its most secret and delicate processes. Propaganda has, in common with all other expression, the object of persuasion; but it pursues that legitimate object by illegitimate means—

by suggestio falsi and suppressio veri; by the argumentum ad hominem and hitting below the belt; by demagogic appeal and the disregard of right reason. The victim of propaganda is not intellectually persuaded, but intellectually—if not emotionally—coerced. The essayist, whatever the limitations of his intelligence, is bound over to be honest; the propagandist is always dishonest.

14 To qualify a large number of the articles and pseudo-essays that appear at present in our serious periodicals, British and American, as "dishonest" calls for a little explaining. When one says that the propagandist is always dishonest, one means this: they are so convinced of the truth of a certain proposition that they dissembles the facts that tell against it. Occasionally, the propogandist is dishonest through ignorance—they are verily unaware of any facts save those that argue for their own position. Sometimes, having approached the subject with this decision already made, they are unable to appreciate the value of hostile facts, even though they are aware of them. In the latter case, instead of presenting those hostile facts fairly, they tend to suppress or distort them because they are afraid that their audience, readers or listeners, will not react to them precisely as they have done. The propagandist believes (when he is not a paid prostitute) that their conclusions are right; but, no more than any other demagogue, do they like to give other men and women a fair chance to decide for themselves. The last thing they will show their reader is Francis of Verulam reasoning with himself. The propogandist cannot encourage the meditative process. They are, at best, the special pleader.

15 It can have escaped no reader of British and American periodicals that there is very little urbane meditation going on in print. Half the articles published are propaganda—political, economic, social; the other half are purely informational, mere catalogs of fact. The essay is nowhere. Either there is no proposition, or evidence is suppressed. Above all, there is no meditation—no urbanity. All this is characteristic of the state of war in which we are unfortunately

living; that state of war which, alas! Permits us few unprejudiced hours.

16 Yet I think many people would agree that we need those unprejudiced hours rather particularly, just now. We need the essay rather particularly, just now, since fiction and poetry have suffered even more cruelly than critical prose from the corruption of propaganda on the one hand and the rage for "fact-finding" on the other. We need to get away from polemics; we even need to get away from statistics. Granted that we are in a state of war: are we positively so badly off that we must permit every sense save the economic to be atrophied; that we cannot afford to think about life in any terms except those of bread? The desperate determination to guarantee bread to every one—which seems to be the basis of all our political and economic quarreling—is perhaps our major duty. And after? As the French say, is it not worth our while to keep ourselves complex and civilized, so that, when bread for every one is guaranteed, we shall be capable of entertaining other interests?

17 The preoccupation with bread alone is a savage's preoccupation; even when it concerns itself altruistically with other people's bread, it is still a savage's preoccupation. The preoccupation with facts to the exclusion of what can be done with them, and the incapacity for logical thinking, are both savage. Until a man begins to think— not merely to lose his temper or to learn by heart—he is, mentally, clothed in the skins of beasts. We are, I fear, under economic stress, de-civilizing ourselves. Between propaganda and "dope" there is little room for the meditative process and the subtler propositions.

18 I am not urging that we play the flute while Rome burns. I recall the sad entry in Dorothy Wordsworth's journal: "William wasted his mind all day in the magazines." I am not asking the magazines to waste the minds of our Williams....The fact that the familiar essay of the whimsical type is not at the moment popular—that when people wish to be diverted, they prefer Wodehouse to Leacock, let us say—does not disturb me. But it seems a pity

that meditative prose should suffer a total eclipse, if only because meditation is highly contagious. A good essay inevitably sets the reader to thinking. Just because it expresses a point of view, is limited by one personality, and cannot be exhaustive or wholly authoritative, it invites the reader to collaboration. A good essay is neither intoxicant nor purge nor anodyne; it is a mental stimulant.

19 Poetry may be, indeed, as Arnold said, "a criticism of life." But most of us need a different training in critical thinking from that which is offered to us by the poets. A vast amount of the detail of life, detail which preoccupies and concerns us all, is left out of great poetry. We do not spend all our time on the heights, or in the depths, and if we are to live we must reflect on many matters rather temporal than eternal. The essayist says, "Come, let us reason together." That is an invitation—whether given by word of mouth or on the printed page—that civilized people must encourage and, as often as possible in their burdened lives, accept.

On Abstract Language

John Pfannkuchen

1   Most things that we read about and talk about exist. But some words, called abstractions, seem like they refer to real things, but they do not. They trick us. They trick writers and readers alike. Abstractions can be useful, but only if you as a writer understand how they work. And if a reader does not understand the difference between what's real and what's abstract they are lost.

2   Ideas, beliefs, events, and processes are abstract. Abstract language often "feels" or seems concrete. But because abstract language cannot be seen or touched this "feeling" of concreteness is not real. However it's not our fault! We confuse abstract and concrete language because the English language treats ideas the same as it does real objects—as nouns. For example: "The Occurrence at Owl Creek Bridge" is about war, or "The Occurrence at Owl Creek Bridge" takes place on a bridge.

3   Look at the nouns "war" and "bridge". Can you tell which noun is concrete and which one is abstract? Both words in the above sentences are nouns. I can stand on a bridge—it is a real physical object. However, I cannot go to the store and buy war, I cannot put war in my pocket. But, you say, I can watch a war unfold on my television. There are certain physical objects that come to mind when you think of the act of war. But these physical things are not the act of war. Bombs, guns, tanks, and soldiers. Our minds may associate various concrete objects with ideas. However, war, by itself, is only an idea, and therefor it is an abstraction.

4   Then what is concrete language? If abstractions are ideas that you cannot experience with the five senses, then concrete things must be just the opposite. Language is said to be concrete if it can be experienced with one or more of the five senses. Concrete

language refers to things, objects and people. Physical things. Payton Faruqar, Owl Creek Bridge, a noose, a river, the water—all of these are words that refer to physical objects. As people or objects concrete language refers to physical things.

5   You'll notice that the specificity and generality of a word plays a role in how abstract or concrete that word is. Words that indicate many things at once, grouped by some kind of logic or character-istic, are called types, stereotypes, classes, or categories. For short I will refer to these as categories. A category in English is language that refers to a collection, class, or type of physical thing. And while the things themselves are concrete, the category, class, or type is abstract. The category is impossible to touch, feel, smell, hear, or see; it is itself an abstract concept. Even though the basis for a cate-gory may be a physical quality that certain concrete objects share, such as color, size, or use. This is the "logic of categorization". And regardless of whether it's concrete or abstract in nature, true or false, doesn't matter. Categorical language plays a key role in propa-ganda and bias—consider a phrase that begins with "all women," or "all Americans" and you'll see what I mean.

6   One cannot experience a category with any of the five senses—it must be thought of. This marks the difference between the cate-gory known simply as saboteur, and a specific saboteur such as Payton Faruqar. When we say that Payton Faruqar is a saboteur, we are really saying that Payton Faruqar belongs to the category of saboteur. But he also belongs to the categories of: man, husband, and victim. But beyond these categories, Payton Faruqar is an indi-vidual, unique and independent from his categories—no thing, much less a person, can be summed up by their categories alone.

7   To expand upon this point, "trees" as a category is somewhat abstract. Many things can be said about "trees" in general, but many more things can be said of certain species of trees (still a cate-gory, but slightly less abstract, less general). And what about that particular tree growing in the park? Everything that can be said of

all trees, and that tree's specie, can be said of it as well. But one can say more about an individual than its categories implies: what sets it apart from the other trees of its categories? Consider its location, its root structure, its health, its ecosystem and the particular creatures that inhabit it (its internal biomes). These are variables that may or may not be true of other trees like of its species, much the entire category of trees.

8   After a certain point generalization, and stereotype, fails us. This point is probably most felt in the realm of characterizing the individual human being. The same processes are in play, and a great writer will understand the dangers of abstraction and choose how much abstraction to and not to use in their topic, question, and hypothesis. They will make this choice deliberately--not accidentally. I am always wary of leaving my argument in the hands of a stereotype, or category.

On Them

Hilaire Belloc

1   I do not like Them. It is no good asking me why, though I have plenty of reasons. I do not like Them. There would be no particular point in saying I do not like Them if it were not that so many people doted on Them, and when one hears Them praised, it goads one to expressing one's hatred and fear of Them.

2   I know very well that They can do one harm, and that They have occult powers. All the world has known that for a hundred thousand years, more or less, and every attempt has been made to propitiate Them. James I. would drown Their mistress or burn her, but They were spared. Men would mummify Them in Egypt, and worship the mummies; men would carve Them in stone in Cyprus, and Crete and Asia Minor, or (more remarkable still) artists, especially in the Western Empire, would leave Them out altogether; so much was Their influence dreaded. Well, I yield so far as not to print Their name, and only to call Them "They", but I hate Them, and I'm not afraid to say so.

3   If you will take a little list of the chief crimes that living beings can commit you will find that They commit them all. And They are cruel; cruelty is even in Their tread and expression. They are hatefully cruel. I saw one of Them catch a mouse the other day (the cat is now out of the bag), and it was a very much more sickening sight, I fancy, than ordinary murder. You may imagine that They catch mice to eat them. It is not so. They catch mice to torture them. And what is worse, They will teach this to Their children— Their children who are naturally innocent and fat, and full of goodness, are deliberately and systematically corrupted by Them; there is diabolism in it.

4   Other beings (I include mankind) will be gluttonous, but glut-

tonous spasmodically, or with a method, or shamefacedly, or, in some way or another that qualifies the vice; not so They. They are gluttonous always and upon all occasions, and in every place and forever. It was only last Vigil of All Fools' Day when, myself fasting, I filled up the saucer seven times with milk and seven times it was emptied, and there went up the most peevish, querulous, vicious complaint and demand for an eighth. They will eat some part of the food of all that are in the house. Now even a child, the most gluttonous one would think of all living creatures, would not do that. It makes a selection, They do not. They will drink beer. This is not a theory; I know it; I have seen it with my own eyes. They will eat special foods; They will even eat dry bread. Here again I have personal evidence of the fact; They will eat the dog's biscuits, but never upon any occasion will They eat anything that has been poisoned, so utterly lacking are They in simplicity and humility, and so abominably well filled with cunning by whatever demon first brought their race into existence.

5   They also, alone of all creation, love hateful noises. Some beings indeed (and I count Man among them) cannot help the voice with which they have been endowed, but they know that it is offensive, and are at pains to make it better; others (such as the peacock or the elephant) also know that their cry is unpleasant. They therefore use it sparingly. Others again, the dove, the nightingale, the thrush, know that their voices are very pleasant, and entertain us with them all day and all night long; but They know that Their voices are the most hideous of all the sounds in the world, and, knowing this, They perpetually insist upon thrusting those voices upon us, saying, as it were, "I am giving myself pain, but I am giving you more pain, and therefore I shall go on." And They choose for the place where this pain shall be given, exact and elevated situations, very close to our ears. Is there any need for me to point out that in every city they will begin their wicked jar just at the time when its inhabitants must sleep? In London you will not hear it till after

midnight; in the county towns it begins at ten; in remote villages as early as nine.

6 Their Master also protects them. They have a charmed life. I have seen one thrown from a great height into a London street, which when It reached it It walked quietly away with the dignity of the Lost World to which It belonged.

7 If one had the time one could watch Them day after day, and never see Them do a single kind or good thing, or be moved by a single virtuous impulse. They have no gesture for the expression of admiration, love, reverence or ecstasy. They have but one method of expressing content, and They reserve that for moments of physical repletion. The tail, which is in all other animals the signal for joy or for defense, or for mere usefulness, or for a noble anger, is with Them agitated only to express a sullen discontent.

8 All that They do is venomous, and all that They think is evil, and when I take mine away (as I mean to do next week—in a basket), I shall first read in a book of statistics what is the wickedest part of London, and I shall leave It there, for I know of no one even among my neighbors quite so vile as to deserve such a gift.

On Bias

John Pfannkuchen

1   Who among us hasn't been asked, at least once, to "choose a thesis, then defend it," or to, "write a thesis driven essay"? When people write this way they usually end up writing propaganda, which is very good for defeating the enemy, but whose truth is questionable at best.

2   I would say that not all biased writing is propaganda, however. I think the main difference is intention. But that doesn't make it any better, mind you. What do I care, when being misled down a dark and dead-end alleyway, if my guide has ill intentions or is merely incompetent? In either case I have been misled. I suppose the principle thing is bias.

3   And what is bias? In my opinion it is somewhat like, but worse than, the blinders they put on horses. Blinders prevent a horse from being spooked, and running off with the cart, while bias might have the same effect on the reader—preventing the reader from getting up and running away from the writer who chooses only to see and share certain aspects of this world, misrepresenting it and misleading us. Bias blots out things before one's eyes, whereas blinders only obscure the peripheral vision.

4   The biased writer forms an opinion without all the facts, and then argues for this opinion by only referencing facts that support this false argument—actively and purposefully avoiding ideas that would cause trouble for their position. In this way bias is not merely "having an opinion," but having an opinion and refusing to change one's proposition regardless of whatever new evidence or ideas one may come across. It is a lazy and dangerous kind of thinking and writing.

5   The biased writer begins with a thesis in mind, and realized

all too late that the thing is due the next morning, and must wrap it up. At this point it is simply easier to lie, dissemble, and avoid inconvenient sources to avoid having to rewrite one's whole argument.

6   The lazy instructor wants the biased writer to produce a "thesis-centered essay" with 3 outside sources. The biased writer will follow their instructions and write the thesis statement first without thinking much about it. After all, the biased writer has been fine up until now, being driven about the streets with a crack whip and blinders on, pulling that cart and being put away dry in their stall every evening.

7   The biased writer must now find 3 sources about their claim. What sources will they choose? If the writer wants to have some free time and get a good grade they'll do as they were told and disregard any inconvenient ideas that don't support their argument!

8   I think the main problem is that because we expect to hear the proposition, or the thesis, at the beginning of the essay—we also expect to write it first as well. But what's stopping an author from writing it last, and merely placing it in the introduction?

9   Most teachers of essay writing nowadays are happy enough to see that the writing student has merely included a thesis (proposition) in their writing, and gone some way to supporting that thesis with "facts." But what teacher has the time and patience to police against spurious logic, and silly arguments, or to make sure the student has considered the issue from all angles, and is prepared to meditate as they write?

10 Sometimes I wonder if it isn't baked into the culture—this resistance to showing any sign of weakness, to showing our work, and revealing our incomplete or partial thoughts and how we got our opinions in the first place: "Write a thesis", they say, "and defend it." But writing isn't combat! Why use words like "defend"? Are we under attack?

11 Instead of thinking of writing as building a fort to protect our precious ideas from invaders, why not instead think of our essays as boxes of sand, in which we can play and dream and have a good time? We make a proposal—construct a sand castle—and show it to the world! Who cares if someone knocks it down, if they replace it with something even cooler? Hey, maybe you can even inspire your reader to make some improvements to your castle.

12 True essay writing requires humility, openness, and meditation—while bias and propaganda require just the opposite—severity, closedness, and an unwillingness to imagine another's perspective.

13 My proposition is to write backwards from the bottom, up; start by reading and thinking, writing lists, and getting inspired by experience and life. Instead of beginning with the proposition and trying to prove it, try reversing the process, and start with the sources. That means reading, thinking, asking questions, and trying out crazy ideas.

14 Once an idea is in hand, you can show it to your reader. Now the essay can be revised, and the proposition placed in the introduction.

15 Voilà!

A Modest Proposal

For preventing the children of poor immigrants from being a burden on their parents or this country, and for making them beneficial to the public.

Jonathan Swift

1   It is a sad sight for those who walk through this great town, or travel in the country, when they see the streets, the roads and front doors crowded with mothers, followed by three, four, or six children, all in rags, and begging for money. These mothers instead of being able to work for their honest livelihood are forced to spend all their time begging for their helpless infants who, as they grow up, either turn to stealing for lack of work, or leave their native country to join a gang, or work themselves into slavery.

2   I think everyone agrees that this is a sad state, and therefore whoever can find a fair, cheap, and easy method of making these children useful citizens would deserve a statue of them erected as a savior of the nation.

3   But I intend to not only provide for the children of immigrants. I have a solution that takes care of a whole number of infants at a certain age who are born to poor parents, like the ones that beg in the streets.

4   I have thought about this for many years, and considered the plans of others in our society. But I have always found these plans mistaken in their computation. It is true that a child just dropped from its mother may be supported by her milk for a year with little other nourishment: for no more than twenty dollars, which the mother could earn by begging. However, at one year old I propose to, instead of allowing them to be a burden upon their parents or the community or needing food and clothing for the rest of their lives, to instead allow the child to contribute to the feeding, and

partly to the clothing, of many thousands.

5 Also there is another great advantage in my plan: it will prevent voluntary abortions, and the horrible practice of women murdering their bastard children. Too often mothers sacrifice poor innocent babies, more to avoid the expense than the shame, which would make the most savage and inhuman person feel pity.

6 There are about one and a half million people in this country. Of these I calculate there may be about two hundred thousand couples whose wives are breeders. From this number I subtract thirty thousand couples, who are able to provide for their children, (although I don't think there are this many, given the state of things) but this being granted, there will remain one hundred and seventy thousand breeders. I again subtract fifty thousand, for those women who miscarry, or for the children who die by accident or disease within the first year. There remains only one hundred and twenty thousand children of poor parents born annually.

7 Therefore the question is: "How will these children be raised, and provided for?" Which I have already said is utterly impossible by all the methods already proposed, as things are now. Because we can neither employ these children in vocational work or agriculture; they can neither build houses, (I mean in the country) nor cultivate land: they can very rarely earn a living by stealing before the age of six. Although I admit they learn the basics much earlier, during which time they can be considered "thieves in training".

8 I am told by our merchants that a boy or a girl before twelve years old cannot be sold, and even when they come to this age, the merchant would not get more than $300 at most on sale; which is not enough to account for even a quarter of the food and clothing needed to raise the child.

9 I shall now therefore humbly propose my own thoughts, which I hope will not be objected to.

10 I have been assured by a very knowing American of my acquain-

tance, that a young healthy child well nursed, is, at a year old, a most delicious nourishing and wholesome food, whether stewed, roasted, baked, or boiled; and I don't doubt that the child would be good in a fricassee, or a ragout.

11 I do therefore humbly offer it to public consideration, that of the hundred and twenty thousand children, that twenty thousand may be reserved for breed, whereas only twenty five percent should be males (which is more than we allow to sheep, black cattle, or swine). My reasoning is that these children are seldom born from marriage, therefore, one male will be sufficient to serve four females.

12 The remaining hundred thousand may, at a year old, be sold to high quality rich people through the country, always advising the mother to let them suck plentifully in the final month to make them plump and fat for a good table. One Haitian child is enough for two dishes at a party with friends, and when the family dines alone, the fore or hind quarter will make a reasonable dish, and seasoned with a little pepper or salt will be very good boiled on the fourth day, especially in winter.

13 I have reckoned that on average a newborn weighing 12 pounds will, in a year, if well nursed, grow to 28 pounds.

14 I grant this food will be somewhat pricey, and therefore very proper for landlords, who, as they have already devoured most of the parents, seem to have the best claim to the children.

15 Infant's flesh will be in season throughout the year, but more plentiful in March, and a little before and after. We are told by a grave author, an eminent French physician, that fish being a popular diet, there are more children born in Roman Catholic countries about nine months after Lent. The markets will be more glutted than usual, because the number of Catholic infants, is at least three to one in this country, and therefore it will have one other collateral advantage, by lessening the number of Catholics among us.

16 I have already computed the cost of nursing a beggar's child (which

includes homesteaders, laborers, and eighty percent of the farmers) to be about ten dollars per year, rags included. And I believe no bachelor would hesitate to pay fifty dollars for the carcass of a good fat child, which would make four dishes of excellent nutritional meat, for when he has a friend or the whole family over for dinner. Therefor the young man will learn to be a good landlord, and grow popular among his tenants, and the mother will have forty dollars profit, and be fit for work till she has another child.

17 Those who are more thrifty (as I must confess the times require) may skin the carcass; the leather of which, when tanned, will make admirable gloves for ladies and summer boots for fine gentlemen.

18 As to Mexico City, butcher houses may be appointed for this purpose, in the most convenient parts of the city, and there will be plenty of work for butchers, although I rather recommend buying the children alive, and dressing them hot from the knife, as we do roasting pigs.

19 A very worthy person, a true lover of his country, and whose virtues I highly esteem, offered a suggestion for my plan. He said that for many gentlemen in this country, having lately hunted all their deer, that their loss of venison might be well replaced by the bodies of young boys and girls, not exceeding fourteen years of age, nor under twelve. This is because there are so many children of this age, both male and female, about to starve for lack of work and jobs, and ready to be gotten rid of by their parents (if alive), or other-wise by their nearest relations. But with due respect to so excel-lent a friend, and so deserving a patriot, I cannot agree with him completely. Because, as for the males, my American acquaintance assured me from experience that their flesh is generally tough and lean, like that of our school-boys, because of continual exercise, and their taste disagreeable, and to fatten them would not make it any better. As for the females, it would be a loss to the public, because they would soon become breeders themselves: and besides, it's likely that some scrupulous people might be willing to say the

practice, (although indeed very unjustly) borders on cruelty, which, I confess, has always been my strongest objection against any project, however well intended.

20 But in order to justify my friend, he confessed, that this idea was put into his head by the famous Salmanaazor, a native of the island Formosa, who had come to London over twenty years ago, and in conversation told my friend, that in his country, when any young person happened to be put to death, the executioner sold the carcass to quality people, as a kind of delicacy; and that, in his time, the body of a plump girl of fifteen, who was crucified for an attempt to poison the Emperor, was sold to his imperial majesty's prime minister of state, and other great mandarins of the court in joints from the gibbet, at four hundred crowns. Neither indeed can I deny, that if the same use were made of several plump young girls in this town, who without one single penny to their names, cannot go abroad without a chair, and appear at a play-house and assemblies in foreign fineries which they never will pay for; the kingdom would not be the worse.

21 Some persons of a desponding spirit are in great concern about that vast number of poor people, who are old, diseased, or handicapped, and I have wondered what course may be taken, to ease the nation of so grievous an issue. But I am not in the least pain upon that matter, because it is very well known, that they are every day dying, and rotting, by cold and famine, and filth, and vermin, as fast as can be reasonably expected. And as to the young workers, they are now in almost as hopeful a condition. They cannot get work, and consequently pine away from lack of food, to a degree, that if at any time they are accidentally hired to common labor, they have not strength to perform it, and thus the country and themselves are happily delivered from the evils to come.

22 I have too long digressed, and therefore shall return to my subject. I think the advantages of my proposal are obvious and many, as well as of the highest importance.

23 For first, as I have already observed, it would greatly lessen the number of Catholics, with whom we are yearly over-run, being the principal breeders of the nation, as well as our most dangerous enemies, and who stay at home on purpose with a design to deliver the country to the enemy, hoping to take their advantage by the absence of so many good Protestants, who have chosen rather to leave their country, than stay at home.

24 Secondly, The poorer tenants will have something valuable of their own, which by law may be made liable to a distress, and help to pay their landlord's rent, their corn and cattle being already seized, and money a thing unknown.

25 Thirdly, Whereas the maintenance of a hundred thousand children, from two years old, and upwards, cannot be computed at less than fifty dollars a piece per annum, the nation's stock will be thereby increased ten million dollars per annum, besides the profit of a new dish, introduced to the tables of all gentlemen of fortune in the country, who have any refinement in taste. And the money will circulate among our selves, the goods being entirely of our own growth and manufacture.

26 Fourthly, The constant breeders, besides the gain of forty dollars profit per annum by the sale of their children, will be rid of the charge of maintaining them after the first year.

27 Fifthly, This food would likewise bring great custom to taverns, where the winemakers will certainly be so prudent as to procure the best receipts for dressing it to perfection, and consequently have their houses frequented by all the fine gentlemen, who justly value themselves upon their knowledge in good eating; and a skillful cook, who understands how to oblige his guests, will contrive to make it as expensive as they please.

28 Sixthly, This would be a great encouragement for marriage, which all wise nations have either encouraged by rewards, or enforced by laws and penalties. It would increase the care and tender-

ness of mothers towards their children, when they were sure of a settlement for life to the poor babes, provided in some sort by the public, to their annual profit instead of expense. We should soon see an honest emulation among the married women, which of them could bring the fattest child to the market. Men would become as fond of their wives, during the time of their pregnancy, as they are now of their mares in foal, their cows in calf, or sow when they are ready to farrow; nor offer to beat or kick them (as is too frequent a practice) for fear of a miscarriage.

29 Many other advantages might be enumerated. For instance, the addition of some thousand carcasses in our exportation of barreled beef, the propagation of swine's flesh, and improvement in the art of making good bacon, so much wanted among us by the great destruction of pigs, too frequent at our tables; which are no way comparable in taste or magnificence to a well grown, fat yearly child, which roasted whole will make a considerable figure at a Lord Mayor's feast, or any other public entertainment. But this, and many others, I omit, being studious of brevity.

30 Supposing that one thousand families in this city, would be constant customers for infants flesh, besides others who might have it at merry meetings, particularly at weddings and christenings, I compute that New York would take off annually about twenty thousand carcasses; and the rest of the kingdom (where probably they will be sold somewhat cheaper) the remaining eighty thousand.

31 I can think of no one objection, that will possibly be raised against this proposal, unless it should be urged, that the number of people will be thereby much lessened in the kingdom. This I freely own, and 'twas indeed one principal design in offering it to the world. I desire the reader will observe, that I calculate my remedy for this one individual country, and for no other that ever was, is, or, I think, ever can be upon Earth. Therefore let no man talk to me of other expedients: of taxing our absentees at 25%: Of using neither

clothes, nor household furniture, except what is of our own growth and manufacture: of utterly rejecting the materials and instruments that promote foreign luxury: of curing the expensiveness of pride, vanity, idleness, and gaming in our women: of introducing a vein of parsimony, prudence and temperance: of learning to love our country, wherein we differ even from Laplanders, and the inhabitants of Topinamboo: of quitting our animosities and factions, nor acting any longer like the Jews, who were murdering one another at the very moment their city was taken: of being a little cautious not to sell our country and consciences for nothing: of teaching landlords to have at least one degree of mercy towards their tenants. Lastly, of putting a spirit of honesty, industry, and skill into our shop-keepers, who, if a resolution could now be taken to buy only our native goods, would immediately unite to cheat and exact upon us in the price, the measure, and the goodness, nor could ever yet be brought to make one fair proposal of just dealing, though often and earnestly invited to it.

32 Therefore I repeat, let no man talk to me of these and or similar ideas until he has at least some idea of how to put them into practice.

33 But, as to my self, having been wearied out for many years with offering vain, idle, visionary thoughts, and at length utterly despairing of success, I fortunately fell upon this proposal, which, as it is wholly new, so it has something solid and real, of no cost and little effort, that we can accomplish alone, and where there is no danger of harming England. For this kind of commodity cannot be exported, since flesh is too tender to transport in salt, although perhaps I could name a country which would be glad to eat up our whole nation without salt.

34 After all, I am not so close-minded that I would reject any offer proposed by wise men that is equally innocent, cheap, easy, and effective. But before I entertain other ideas I want the author or authors to consider two points. First, ss things now stand, how will

they find food and clothing for a hundred thousand useless mouths and backs? And secondly, There a million creatures in human figure throughout this kingdom, who cost the kingdom two million pounds sterling, adding those who are beggars by profession, to the bulk of farmers, homesteaders and laborers, with their wives and children, who are beggars in effect; I desire those politicians who dislike my ideas, and think they have a better idea, that they will first ask the parents of these mortals, whether they would not today want to have been sold for food at a year old, in the manner I suggest, and therefor having avoided all the misfortunes they have experienced, by the oppression of landlords, the impossibility of paying rent without money or work, the lack of common food, with neither house nor clothes to cover them from the weather, and the most inevitable prospect of inflicting the same or worse miseries upon their kind for ever?

35 I profess, in the sincerity of my heart, that I have no personal interest in trying to promote this necessary work, having no other motive than the public good of my country, by advancing our trade, providing for infants, relieving the poor, and giving some pleasure to the rich. I have no children, by which I can propose to get a single penny; the youngest being nine years old, and my wife past child-bearing.

What is a Fact?

John Pfannkuchen

"...With a little practice you will see far better than those who quarrel about the shadows, whose knowledge is a dream only, whilst yours is a waking reality."

Plato

1   What is a fact? Most people I talk to seem to regard facts as little gods that they can carry around in their pockets and present at any opportune time, like say in argument, or to impress strangers. "Did you know...?" one starts off, "It's a fact that..." and on they drone, with authority.

2   Most people in our modern age have come to believe that facts are merely the truth, itemized. But sometimes, when I am being assaulted by a rather heavy torrent of facts, I begin to wonder if it's not so? I wonder if humans actually don't know the truth. So on this point I propose to discuss the difference between truth and fact.

3   A fact is what is known or proved to be true. Let's reflect on that for a moment. It's what's known to be or proven to be true. It's not true per say. Long story short, a fact is what people think is true at the time. What's a fact one minute could be old fashioned or backward thinking the next. If human knowledge is composed purely of facts, then, isn't it incomplete or simply wrong? I think so—but if that's the case, why do we build these sandcastles and cards of houses out of so many facts, just for the tide to come in and displace it all? I think facts are humanity's way of admitting we cannot possible know the truth, but settling for the next best thing anyways. To function human society needs something to rely on, some knowledge to base our decisions on—society is the act of cohabitation, or living together, and how difficult it would be to

live with a bunch of people with which we disagree on everything!

4   And how do we establish facts, create them, manufacture, and publish them to the minds of men? I believe we can, ever since the Enlightenment, look toward science for the answers on scientific facts (what is demonstrated to always be true), but there are other kinds of facts as well, like historical facts (what we believe to have happened).

5   In these cases facts must be demonstrated—and not just once either—but in science the cause and effect that produced a fact must be reliably reproduced by different scientists. Consider the fact of gravity—and how it became a fact, and how humankind had gravity sewn up as "what goes up must come down" for so long, until a guy named Einstein came along and offered us his general theory of relativity.

6   "Well," you say, "what's the practical difference between truth and fact?" The practical difference between truth and fact is this: every day a fact is proven either partially or entirely wrong, and either changed, or entirely replaced by some newer, more correct fact. This is what we call "scientific progress."

7   Facts change. Facts are knowable. But the truth? The truth never changes. And we may never know it, and if we do know it, we can never know that we do know it. That's the implication of truth versus fact!

8   If an essayist understands that ultimate truth is beyond the grasp of human understanding—many possibilities are open to them—not least of which is the questioning of certain facts. Because—think of it! What a dull world we would live in if every child's imagination, and every artist's brush, and every writer's pen only held to known facts! What horrible science we would have— no science at all, really—if all people were satisfied with what they were told!

9   The essayist must question the facts of their society like grains of

sand, pack them with water and make shapes of them, and wait for the tide to come and rearrange them once more, taking some out to sea, leaving others as a jumbled mess on the beach.

Of Truth

Francis Bacon

1   The official who presided over the trial of Jesus Christ and ordered his crucifixion asked in jest, "What is truth?" He did not stay for the answer. Certainly there are people that delight in giddiness, and consider it important to believe in something, affecting free will in thinking as well as in acting. And though those philosophers are gone, there are still similar people who believe the same thing, though there's not as much blood in them as was in those of the ancients.

2   But it is not only the difficulty and labor which men take in finding out the truth, nor the imposition upon men's thoughts that favors lying, but a natural though corrupt love of the lie itself.

3   One of the later Greek schools examines the matter and concludes that men love lying, whether they do it for pleasure as with poets, or for profit as with the merchant; they lie for the lie's sake. But I cannot tell; the answer is a naked and open daylight that does not show the masks and mummeries and triumphs of the world half so stately and daintily as candlelight.

4   Truth may be the price of a pearl that looks best during the day, but it's not worth the price of a diamond that looks best in any light. A mixture of a lie always adds pleasure. Does anyone doubt that if vain opinions, flattering hopes, false valuations, imaginations, and the like were taken out of men's minds, that it would leave their minds poor shrunken things, full of melancholy and indisposition, and unpleasing to themselves?

5   One of the fathers, in great severity, called poetry "vinum dæmonum" [devils' wine], because it fills the imagination, and yet it contains the shadow of a lie. But it is not the lie that passes through the mind that does damage, but the lie that sinks in and settles. But

regardless of how these things are in men's depraved judgments and affections, truth, which only judges itself, teaches that the search for truth (the flirting or wooing of it), the knowledge of truth (the presence of it), and the belief of truth (which is the enjoying of it), is the sovereign good of human nature. No other creature can know the truth like humankind.

6   The first creature of God, in the works of the days, was the light of the sense; the last was the light of reason, and ever since his work on the Sabbath has illuminated his Spirit. First God breathes light upon the face of chaos, then he breathes light into the face of man, and still he breathes and inspires light into the face of his chosen.

7   A poet once said that it is a pleasure to stand upon the shore and to see ships tossed upon the sea, a pleasure to stand in the window of a castle and to see a battle and the adventures thereof below: but no pleasure is comparable to standing upon the vantage ground of truth (a hill is unnecessary where the air is always clear and serene), and to see the errors and wanderings and mists and tempests in the vale below, so long as this position is taken with pity, and not with swelling or pride.

8   Certainly it is heaven upon earth to have a man's mind move in charity, rest in providence, and turn upon the poles of truth. To pass from theological and philosophical truth to the truth of civil business, it would be admitted even by those who don't practice it that clear and round dealing is the honor of man's nature, and that mixture of falsehood is like alloy in coin of gold and silver, which may make the metal stronger and lighter but corrupts it. For these winding and crooked courses are the goings of the serpent, which moves basely upon the belly and not upon the feet. There is no vice that covers a man with so much shame as being called false and untrustworthy.

9   And therefore Montaigne said prettily, when he asked why lying should be such a disgrace and such an odious accusation, that if you think about it, "to say that a man lies is to say that he is brave

towards God and a coward towards men," because a lie faces God and shrinks from man. Surely the wickedness of falsehood and breach of faith shall be the last judgment of God upon the generations of men; it being foretold that when Christ comes he will not find faith upon the earth.

Allegory of the Cave

Plato

1 And now I will describe in a metaphor the enlightenment or unen-
lightenment of our nature: Imagine humans living in an underground cave which is open towards the light. They have been there
since childhood with their necks and legs chained, and can see only
into the cave.

2 At a distance there is a fire, and between the fire and the prisoners
a raised way, and a low wall is built along the way, like a movie
screen. Behind the screen appear moving figures who hold in their
hands various works of art, and among them images of men and
animals, wood and stone, and some of the passers-by are talking
and others silent.

3 "A strange story, and strange captives."

4 But they are ourselves, I reply, and they see only the images which
the light throws on the screen; to these they give names, and if we
add an echo which returns from the wall, the voices of the passen-
gers will seem to proceed from the shadows. Suppose now that you
suddenly turn them round and make them look with pain and
grief at real things; will they believe them to be real?

5 Will not their eyes be dazzled, and will they not try to get away
from the light to something which they are able to see without
blinking? And suppose further, that they are dragged up a steep and
rugged ascent into the presence of the sun—will not their sight be
darkened with the excess of light?

6 Some time will pass before their eyes adjust, and at first they will
be able to see only shadows and reflections in the water; then they
will recognize the moon and the stars, and will at length see the sun
in its proper place.

7 Last of all they will conclude: "This is that which gives us the year

and the seasons, and is the author of all that we see." How will they rejoice in passing from darkness to light! How worthless to them will seem the honors and glories of the cave!

8 But now imagine further, that they descend into their old home—in that underground dwelling they will not see as well as their fellows, and will not be able to compete with them in the measurement of the shadows on the wall. There will be many jokes about the man who went on a visit to the sun and lost his eyes! And if they find anybody trying to set free and enlighten one of their number, they will put him to death, if they can catch him.

9 Now the cave is the world of sight, the fire is the sun, the way upwards is the way to knowledge, and in the world of knowledge the idea of good is the very last thing seen, and with difficulty, but when seen it is inferred to be the author of good and right—parent of the lord of light in this world, and of truth and understanding in the other.

10 He who attains the beatiful vision is always going upwards; he is unwilling to descend into political assemblies and courts of law, because his eyes tend to blink at the images or shadows of images before him—he cannot enter into the ideas of those who have never in their lives understood the relation of the shadow to the substance.

11 But blindness is of two kinds, and may be caused either by passing out of darkness into light or out of light into darkness, and a man of sense will distinguish between them, and will not laugh equally at both of them, instead the blindness which arises from fullness of light he will consider blessed, and he will pity the other; or if he laughs at the puzzled people looking at the sun, he will have more reason to laugh than did the inhabitants of the cave at those who came from above.

12 There is a further lesson taught by this parable of ours. Some persons fancy that teaching is like giving eyes to the blind, but we say that

the faculty of sight was always there, and that the soul only requires to be turned round towards the light. And this is conversion; other virtues are almost like bodily habits, and may be acquired in the same manner, but intelligence has a diviner life, and is indestructible, turning either to good or evil according to the direction given. Did you never observe how the mind of a clever conman peers out of his eyes, and the more clearly he sees, the more evil he does? Now if you take someone like this, and cut away from him those leaden weights of pleasure and desire which bind his soul to earth, his intelligence will be turned round, and he will behold the truth as clearly as he now discerns his meaner ends.

13 And have we not decided that our rulers must neither be so uneducated as to have no fixed rule of life, nor so over-educated as to be unwilling to leave their paradise for the business of the world? We must therefore choose the natures who are most likely to ascend to the light and knowledge of the good, but we must not allow them to remain in the region of light—they must be forced down again among the captives in the cave to do their work and and win their honors.

14 "Will they not think this a hardship?" You should remember that our purpose in framing the State was not that our citizens should do what they like, but that they should serve the State for the common good of all. May we not fairly say to our philosopher, "Friend, we do you no wrong; for in other States philosophy grows wild, and a wild plant owes nothing to the gardener, but you have been trained by us to be the rulers and kings of our hive, and therefore we must insist on your descending into the cave." You must, each of you, take your turn, and become able to use your eyes in the dark, and with a little practice you will see far better than those who quarrel about the shadows, whose knowledge is a dream only, while yours is a waking reality.

15 It may be that the saint or philosopher who is the best fit may also be the least inclined to rule, but necessity is laid upon him, and he

must no longer live in the heaven of ideas.

16 And this will be the salvation of the State. Because those who rule must not be those who want to rule; and, if you can offer to our citizens a better life than that of rulers, there will be a chance that the rich, not only in this world's goods, but in virtue and wisdom, may bear rule. And the only life which is better than the life of political ambition is that of philosophy, which is also the best preparation for the government of a State.

On Readers

John Pfannkuchen

1 I try to imagine the reader—a person, I presume, or perhaps a very learned pet, that has gotten hold of its master's bookshelf. But what is the character of the entity, whether it be animal, vegetable, mineral, or other? As an essayist, I put pen to paper, and wonder "Who will read this? A passing stranger? A close relation?"

2 I can imagine and guess, and build magnificent profiles of the people for whom these essays have been penned—but that's not the exercise of this essay, nor is it the point. I will admit that it is probably impossible to say with certainty for whom an essay was written, unless named directly by the author. Even then it might be a lie.

3 But it's my proposition that, for every good essay, that there was a someone out there somewhere for whom it was written specifically. Not just "people in general," or a "certain kind of person." No—there must have been an image of the person for whom it was written burned into the essay.

4 It seems that in some essays the writer is very passionate about their subject, and in others the writer seems to only follow some minute and fleeting strand of logic, like a child running through the forest. In some essays the writing is familiar and comfortable, focused and clean; in others it is meandering, unsure of itself, and widely varied in scope. It is because of some reader, the knowledge of this reader, that the essayist can know exactly how to write—because of the anticipation of this reader, a thousand questions have been answered without needing to be asked! Questions on style, substance, focus, language, scope, language, and more.

5 When one writes for a reader the fact cannot be escaped. It may be a close relation, known for years, like a sibling, a parent, or a lover,

or a childhood friend, or a passing acquaintance, someone met at a party or a cafe once, and with whom was shared a very engaging argument, or a stranger on the street that was stood in line with to buy lunch—or the vendor himself. The writer cannot help but to be haunted by the person and situation for whom the writing applies, to imagine certain qualities of their character. The writing could even be for someone whom the essayist has never personally met someone on the news—the President of the United States, a Syrian refugee, a man who rescued puppies from a burning pet store, a woman who puts chocolate syrup on hot dogs. But why?

6   I have decided that it's important to bear someone in mind, to write for someone, when penning an essay. Here is why:

7   1. The essay becomes more particular than general—by choosing a person to write for, the essayist should also choose a reason for writing for this person. This reason has bound up in it the essayist's memory of the person. This memory, and reason for the essayist's memory, lends itself to a topic.

8   2. The essay becomes more interesting to the essayist—by choosing something that has resided in memory, the essayist can count on there being some emotional connection to that memory, because after all there is likely a reason they remembered it, even if they're unsure of what that reason is. The essayist will discover, by layers, and stages, and through very careful and delicate investigation, why this memory has stayed with them.

9   3. The essayist knows how to write "for" that person—many writers struggle with the question of what level of language is appropriate to use for their essays. They fuss over first person, second person, or third person. They worry about contractions like "isn't, wasn't, and aren't." But when one writes for someone they need only draw on their impression of that person, and their purpose for writing for them, to guide them in these decisions.

10 4. The essay has a purpose, instead of being purposeless.

11 5. The essay has a built-in audience! The beauty of writing for a particular person is that there are likely one hundred thousand people like that one person, and in that case at least a billion people who either know or have heard of someone similar to the person that is being written for. In other words, when one writes for only one particular person the opposite thing happens: their work becomes more relatable!

12 In this list of benefits we find some guidelines as well, for whom we shouldn't write for. Many a first year essayist will take the lazy route and try to write "for their instructor." This can and could work, unless of course one feels absolutely no passion regarding their instructor. If one has no specific memories on which to draw, if an essayist has no disagreement, or message to convey, or encouragement to offer—if indeed the essayist has no memory whatsoever that sticks in their mind—then writing for their instructor should not be a first choice.

13 The essayist must think of someone for whom they can write for. Someone who has left a lasting impression on them, if only in passing. It is this impression the essayist draws on.

14 But! You cry, it is very well and good to write for a particular person—but what if I want my writing to be readable by a general audience? Well then, I reply, look at any professionally published essay and ask yourself if it is passable, if you can or cannot relate to the author, if you have learned nothing valuable, or if you enjoyed the time you spent reading.

15 It is true; in the end an essayist may need to change their work in small degrees to meet certain requirements—for publication, or merely for a writing instructor—but that is a question of process. I believe it is best to begin with someone particular in mind, and if other people must be taken into consideration, let them guide the editing long after the first draft is complete, and only if it is absolutely necessary.

On Introductions

John Pfannkuchen

1   I avoid the moment—with all its falsity and pomp. I never shake hands, except when playing with dogs, and making introductions. I also find looking people in the eyes, smiling, and pretending that I didn't wish to be on a couch somewhere somewhat dishonest. Sometimes I have the opportunity to meet someone very interesting, but in these cases an introduction is altogether forgotten in place of some interesting circumstance or conversation that seems to have arisen between myself and the stranger, like the spark of a wildfire. Eventually we may get to exchanging names, but the anxiety is mostly gone; replaced by a tacit and felt interest in whatever caused us to converse in the first place—and perhaps a shared interest in the other person. In this way chance encounters are the bread and butter of a happy life, while the sideshow of being introduced to a mutual acquaintance—someone we had no choice in meeting, with forced interest, is a form of torture.

2   I harbor the suspicion, the theory, that introductions in writing can be just as pleasant and interesting and invigorating as chance encounters with interesting, like minded people—or they can go the opposite way as well. But introductions in writing aren't by chance from the writer's perspective. The essayist has set out to introduce something, and it's a chance as to whether or not an interested party will pick it up and read it.

3   Now we must ask ourselves this question: what is the point of an introduction? Why not just throw something down and call it a day? Let the reader figure out which way is up, and which way down?

4   The typical answer is because when we take the time to consider the reader, we have to admit that it might be terribly confus-

ing to have no introduction whatsoever—or would it? If I were to merely launch into a heady discussion of material science with an eight year girl in the jelly bean store, would I be well received, by her or her legal guardians, much less the store clerks? In this case, I'm not sure an introduction could save me—I have chosen the wrong audience for my thoughts.

5   But if I were standing before a microprocessor fabrication plant, with a class of fellow physicists, would an introduction be necessary? Some of my fellows might get the idea that, since we are equals, and they already are familiar with the facts, that I am talking down to them, and wasting their time. But for politeness sake they would be obligated to stand and nod, and wait to be let out for recess.

6   But let's say that the reader and I have something in common, and we are on the verge of discovering this something at the same time. That feels more like a chance encounter—an insight shared by two people.

7   In this case, let me make a proposition, that the whole point, then, of an introduction, is to get the reader from the title to the main content of your essay. If your introduction doesn't add something, then it shouldn't exist; it's redundant, and all things redundant have no business being printed onto dead trees, and passed on to unwitting passersby.

8   So what purpose could an introduction possibly have, there sandwiched between the title and the body of your essay?

9   The one idea that often gets lost in most discussions of essay writing is how fun an introduction could, should, and ought to be. Most people open up with a bland, if not downright eye-wateringly boring segue from the most general. Some examples of bad writing

include:

1. Defining a Word or Concept (that the reader already understands).

2. Introducing the Topic (that the reader should already be familiar with).

3. Anything that starts with or contains the words: "Throughout History..."

4. Silly rhetorical questions: "Have you ever wondered...?"

10 Many writers make the mistake of thinking they must begin their essays with a general, or vague introduction. One of the reasons this happens are because the writer doesn't know a few things. They don't know:

1. Who they're writing for (Reader).

2. What they're writing for (Purpose).

11 So their introduction can't possibly be anything but general, since it's an introduction for literally everyone and for every possible purpose. It's a natural thing to speak in general, and to use dictionary definitions to fluff up such an introduction. But this makes for horribly bad writing—because it does the opposite of what an introduction is supposed to do, which is get the reader from the title to the body of your essay. A poorly written, vague, bland, and boring introduction will stop the reader in their tracks, and have them reaching for some other writer who knows who they're writing for and why.

Goldfish

A. A. Milne

1   Let us talk about—well, anything you will. Goldfish, for instance.

2   Goldfish are a symbol of old-world tranquility or mid-Victorian futility according to their position in the home. Outside the home, in that wild state from which civilization has dragged them, they may have stood for dare-devil courage or constancy or devotion; I cannot tell. I may only speak of them now as I find them, which is in the garden or in the drawing-room. In their lily-leaved pool, sunk deep in the old flagged terrace, upon whose borders the blackbird whistles his early-morning song, they remind me of sundials and lavender and old delightful things. But in their cheap glass bowl upon the three-legged table, above which the cloth-covered canary maintains a stolid silence, they remind me of antimacassars and horsehair sofas and all that is depressing. It is hard that the goldfish himself should have so little choice in the matter. Goldfish look pretty in the terrace pond, yet I doubt if it was the need for prettiness which brought them there. Rather the need for some thing to throw things to. No one of the initiate can sit in front of Nature's most wonderful effect, the sea, without wishing to throw stones into it, the physical pleasure of the effort and the aesthetic pleasure of the splash combining to produce perfect contentment. So by the margin of the pool the same desires stir within one, and because ants' eggs do not splash, and look untidy on the surface of the water, there must be a gleam of gold and silver to put the crown upon one's pleasure.

3   Perhaps when you have been feeding the goldfish you have not thought of it like that. But at least you must have wondered why, of all diets, they should prefer ants' eggs. Ants' eggs are, I should say, the very last thing which one would take to without argument. It must be an acquired taste, and, this being so, one naturally asks

oneself how goldfish came to acquire it.

4　I suppose (but I am lamentably ignorant on these as on all other matters) that there was a time when goldfish lived a wild free life of their own. They roamed the sea or the river, or whatever it was, fighting for existence, and Nature showed them, as she always does, the food which suited them. Now I have often come across ants' nests in my travels, but never when swimming. In seas and rivers, pools and lakes, I have wandered, but Nature has never put ants' eggs in my way. No doubt—it would be only right—the goldfish has a keener eye than I have for these things, but if they had been there, should I have missed them so completely? I think not, for if they had been there, they must have been there in great quantities. I can imagine a goldfish slowly acquiring the taste for them through the centuries, but only if other food were denied to him, only if, wherever he went, ants' eggs, ants' eggs, ants' eggs drifted down the stream to him.

5　Yet, since it would seem that he has acquired the taste, it can only be that the taste has come to him with captivity—has been forced upon him, I should have said. The old wild goldfish (this is my theory) was a more terrible beast than we think. Given his proper diet, he could not have been kept within the limits of the terrace pool. He would have been unsuited to domestic life; he would have dragged in the shrieking child as she leaned to feed him. As the result of many experiments ants' eggs were given him to keep him thin (you can see for yourself what a bloodless diet it is), ants' eggs were given him to quell his spirit; and just as a man, if he has sufficient colds, can get up a passion even for ammoniated quinine, so the goldfish has grown in captivity to welcome the once-hated omelet.

6　Let us consider now the case of the goldfish in the house. His diet is the same, but how different his surroundings! If his bowl is placed on a table in the middle of the floor, he has but to flash his tail once and he has been all round the drawing-room. The drawing-room may not seem much to you, but to him this impressionist picture through the curved glass must be amazing. Let not the outdoor goldfish boast of his freedom. What does he, in his little world of water-lily roots, know of the vista upon vista which opens to his more happy brother as he passes jauntily from china dog to ottoman and from ottoman to Henry's father? Ah, here is life! It may be that in the course of years he will get used to it, even bored by it; indeed, for that reason I always advocate giving him a glance at the dining-room or the bedrooms on Wednesdays and Saturdays; but his first day in the bowl must be the opening of an undreamed-of heaven to him.

7 Again, what an adventurous life is his. At any moment a cat may climb up and fetch him out, a child may upset him, grown-ups may neglect to feed him or to change his water. The temptation to take him up and massage him must be irresistible to outsiders. All these dangers the goldfish in the pond avoids; he lives a sheltered and unexciting life, and when he wants to die he dies unnoticed, unregretted, but for his brother the tears and the solemn funeral.

8 Yes; now that I have thought it out, I can see that I was wrong in calling the indoor goldfish a symbol of mid-Victorian futility. An article of this sort is no good if it does not teach the writer something as well as his readers. I recognize him now as the symbol of enterprise and endurance, of restlessness and Post-Impressionism. He is not mid-Victorian, he is Fifth Georgian.

9 Which is all I want to say about goldfish.

Assertion and Support

John Pfannkuchen

1 I often find myself in the company of people who just say things, and am left with the distinct impression that everyone beside myself might actually believe it. There seems to be a reticence toward the idea of challenge, or question-asking in these circumstances, or perhaps it's merely the motive of self preservation on the part of the listener, not wanting to put their foot into something they might not well get out of. I can sympathize. But with the person doing the speaking, making bold assertions, like, "The economy is doing great," and any statements with "Western Culture" as the subject, or that begin with "Throughout time," or "I read a study," and the like. Hopelessly vague, unattributed, and unaccountable are the impressions left on me. Now—I know what you're thinking—I'm a terrible conversationalist. And that's probably true, and anyways, what does it matter where I got the thing I'm saying to you now? So long as one of us is convinced of its veracity.

2 Well dear reader—I will tell you—sometimes people say ridiculous things for affect, and other times people say ridiculous things dressed up as reasonable; I believe that the ability to just say a thing without reason or evidence has all but ruined regular conversation. People will just say anything nowadays, including perfectly contradictory things in the same breath, and it's fine because no one is listening anyway. That's the real casualty of meaningless talk—the loss of interest—no one wants to listen to anyone anymore because as I previous stated, people "just talk", making sounds with their mouths, more or less without intention or purpose.

3 In writing it is the same as in speaking. In writing we call it a thesis—and in speaking a proposition. I believe that one should think before they speak, so it follows that one should think before they write. Which means that if one is to form a thesis in writing,

it should be formed after the bulk of the essay has already been written, so that the writing itself will buy the essayist time to make up their mind.

4   By the way, even in writing I prefer the word proposition to thesis, since both words mean the same thing, but while proposition is clear English, the other is pompous and technical sounding, and tends to send one into fits.

5   A proposition differs from an assertion in that it is felt less strongly than an assertion, that is, the author admits that it is a merely a proposition, and not a fact. However, in the offering of a proposition, the essayist will have the opportunity to make certain assertions of fact, opinion, or observation, in support of their proposition. The way I remember it is this: propositions are supported by assertions; assertions are supported by facts; and facts are supported by observation.

6   So, let's say I read something. And I see or experienced something. And the thing I read, or the memory I have, gives me an idea. Well, I need a way of telling the reader about the connection between my experience and my idea, don't I?

7   So I assert an idea. This is where I get into trouble. I have said something bold, that the reader may find surprising or silly. Can't I just leave it at that, and expect you, my dear reader, to trust in my words? I don't even feel the need to show you how I came upon this idea, but instead I offer to spend a few hundred words repeating in various ways that I am definitely right, trustworthy, and anyone who dare doubt me is a nincompoop or a Communist.

8   But I don't think my tactics will hold water for long. I've learned to assume that even quiet and agreeable people, when reading or listening, will wonder quietly, "Is that true? How do you know?" So I've gotten into the habit of explaining myself, so as not to leave the reader with the impression that I should always be believed at face value (I am often wrong).

9 So I've gotten into the habit of sharing how I had came up with the proposition in the first place, starting from the original observation that was made, and then moving through the assertions, and finally to my proposition, showing the entire chain of logic and deduction to the reader. I try to lay this all out quite methodically. The support can come in any form, really. It can be reasoning, a reference to something we read or saw or a historical fact. It can be anything. But I have to support my assertions somehow.

10 It may be enough for some to just assault the poor reader with assertion after assertion, until the reader waves a white flag of surrender; and although I believe many great writers may wear the reader down, convince the reader to accept any proposition made with little to no convincing other than sheer force of personality, it hasn't worked for me yet.

On Getting Respected in Inns and Hotels

Hilaire Belloc

1   To begin at the beginning is, next to ending at the end, the whole art of writing; as for the middle you may fill it in with any rubble that you choose. But the beginning and the end, like the strong stone outer walls of medieval buildings, contain and define the whole.

2   And there is more than this: since writing is a human and a living art, the beginning being the motive and the end the object of the work, each inspires it; each runs through organically, and the two between them give life to what you do.

3   So I will begin at the beginning and I will lay down this first principle, that religion and the full meaning of things has nowhere more disappeared from the modern world than in the department of Guide Books.

4   For a Guide Book will tell you always what are the principal and most vulgar sights of a town; what mountains are most difficult to climb, and, invariably, the exact distances between one place and another. But these things do not serve the End of Man. The end of man is Happiness, and how much happier are you with such a knowledge? Now there are some Guide Books which do make little excursions now and then into the important things, which tell you (for instance) what kind of cooking you will find in what places, what kind of wine in countries where this beverage is publicly known, and even a few, more daring than the rest, will give a hint or two upon hiring mules, and upon the way that a bargain should be conducted, or how to fight.

5   But with all this even the best of them do not go to the moral heart

of the matter. They do not give you a hint or an idea of that which is surely the basis of all happiness in travel. I mean, the art of gaining respect in the places where you stay. Unless that respect is paid you, you are more miserable by far than if you had stayed at home, and I would ask anyone who reads this whether he can remember one single journey of his which was not marred by the evident contempt which the servants and the owners of taverns showed for him wherever he went?

6   It is therefore of the first importance, much more important than any question of price or distance, to know something of this art; it is not difficult to learn, moreover it is so little exploited that if you will but learn it you will have a sense of privilege and of upstanding among your fellows worth all the holidays which were ever taken in the world.

7   Of this Respect which we seek, out of so many human pleasures, a facile, and a very false interpretation is that it is the privilege of the rich, and I even knew one poor fellow who forged a check and went to gaol [jail] in his desire to impress the host of the "Spotted Dog," near Barnard Castle. It was an error in him, as it is in all who so imagine. The rich in their degree fall under this contempt as heavily as any, and there is no wealth that can purchase the true awe which it should be your aim to receive from waiters, serving-wenches, boot-blacks, and publicans.

8   I knew a man once who set out walking from Oxford to Stow-in-the-Wold, from Stow-in-the-Wold to Cheltenham, from Cheltenham to Ledbury, from Ledbury to Hereford, from Hereford to New Rhayader (where the Cobbler lives), and from New Rhayader to the end of the world which lies a little west and north of that place, and all the way he slept rough under hedges and in stacks, or by day in open fields, so terrified was he at the thought of the contempt that awaited him should he pay for a bed. And I knew another man who walked from York to Thirsk, and from Thirsk to Darlington, and from Darlington to Durham, and so on up to the

border and over it, and all the way he pretended to be extremely poor so that he might be certain the contempt he received was due to nothing of his own, but to his clothes only: but this was an indifferent way of escaping, for it got him into many fights with miners, and he was arrested by the police in Lanchester; and at Jedburgh, where his money did really fail him, he had to walk all through the night, finding that no one would take in such a tatterdemalion. The thing could be done much more cheaply than that, and much more respectably, and you can acquire with but little practice one of many ways of achieving the full respect of the whole house, even of that proud woman who sits behind glass in front of an enormous ledger; and the first way is this:—

9   As you come into the place go straight for the smoking-room, and begin talking of the local sport: and do not talk humbly and tentatively as so many do, but in a loud authoritative tone. You shall insist and lay down the law and fly into a passion if you are contradicted. There is here an objection which will arise in the mind of every niggler and boggler who has in the past very properly been covered with ridicule and become the butt of the waiters and stable-yard, which is, that if one is ignorant of the local sport, there is an end to the business. The objection is ridiculous. Do you suppose that the people whom you hear talking around you are more learned than yourself in the matter? And if they are do you suppose that they are acquainted with your ignorance? Remember that most of them have read far less than you, and that you can draw upon an experience of travel of which they can know nothing; do but make the plunge, practicing first in the villages of the Midlands, I will warrant you that in a very little while bold assertion of this kind will carry you through any tap-room or bar-parlour in Britain.

10 I remember once in the holy and secluded village of Washington under the Downs, there came in upon us as we sat in the inn there a man whom I recognized though he did not know me—for a journalist—incapable of understanding the driving of a cow, let

alone horses: a prophet, a socialist, a man who knew the trend of things and so forth: a man who had never been outside a town except upon a motor bicycle, upon which snorting beast indeed had he come to this inn. But if he was less than us in so many things he was greater than us in this art of gaining respect in Inns and Hotels. For he sat down, and when they had barely had time to say good day to him he gave us in minutest detail a great run after a fox, a run that never took place. We were fifteen men in the room; none of us were anything like rich enough to hunt, and the lie went through them like an express. This fellow "found" (whatever that may mean) at Gumber Corner, ran right through the combe (which, by the way, is one of those bits of land which have been stolen bodily from the English people), cut down the Sutton Road, across the railway at Coates (and there he showed the cloven hoof, for your liar always takes his hounds across the railway), then all over Egdean, and killed in a field near Wisborough. All this he told, and there was not even a man there to ask him whether all those little dogs and horses swam the Rother or jumped it. He was treated like a god; they tried to make him stop but he would not. He was off to Worthing, where I have no doubt he told some further lies upon the growing of tomatoes under glass, which is the main sport of that district. Similarly, I have no doubt, such a man would talk about boats at King's Lynn, murder with violence at Croydon, duck shooting at Ely, and racing anywhere.

11 Then also if you are in any doubt as to what they want of you, you can always change the scene. Thus fishing is dangerous for even the poor can fish, and the chances are you do not know the names of the animals, and you may be putting salt-water fish into the stream of Lambourne, or talking of salmon upon the Upper Thames. But what is to prevent you putting on a look of distance and marvel, and conjuring up the North Atlantic for them? Hold them with the cold and the fog of the Newfoundland seas, and terrify their simple minds with whales.

12 A second way to attain respect, if you are by nature a silent man, and one which I think is always successful, is to write before you go to bed and leave upon the table a great number of envelopes which you should address to members of the Cabinet, and Jewish money-lenders, dukes, and in general any of the great. It is but slight labor, and for the contents you cannot do better than put into each envelope one of those advertisements which you will find lying about. Then next morning you should gather them up and ask where the post is: but you need not post them, and you need not fear for your bill. Your bill will stand much the same, and your reputation will swell like a sponge.

13 And a third way is to go to the telephone, since there are telephones nowadays, and ring up whoever in the neighborhood is of the greatest importance. There is no law against it, and when you have the number you have but to ask the servant at the other end whether it is not somebody else's house. But in the meanwhile your night in the place is secure.

14 And a fourth way is to tell them to call you extremely early, and then to get up extremely late. Now why this should have the effect it has I confess I cannot tell. I lay down the rule empirically and from long observation, but I may suggest that perhaps it is the combination of the energy you show in early rising, and of the luxury you show in late rising: for energy and luxury are the two qualities which menials most admire in that governing class to which you flatter yourself you belong. Moreover the strength of will with which you sweep aside their inconvenience, ordering one thing and doing another, is not without its effect, and the stir you have created is of use to you.

15 And the fifth way is to be Strong, to Dominate and to Lead. To be one of the Makers of this world, one of the Builders. To have the more Powerful Will. To arouse in all around you by mere Force of Personality a feeling that they must Obey. But I do not know how this is done.

Conclusions

John Pfannkuchen

1   As I finish reading the essay Hilaire Belloc's "On Getting Respected in Inns and Hotels," I find myself wondering: where is the conclusion? Where does it begin? Then I wonder, how did it make me feel? If I search my feelings, maybe that will be a clue as to where the essayist begins concluding. Perhaps it's at the beginning of the final paragraph: "And the fifth way is to be Strong, to Dominate and to Lead." This makes little sense, as a topic sentence for a concluding paragraph, because the sentences before them merely enumerated the other ways of "Getting Respect." No, if I were to merely glance at this essay, I would conclude that the conclusion is either very abrupt, well hidden, very long or very short, or some combination of these. On the possibility of the conclusion being long, I search and find that the paragraph before begins with "Then also if you are in any doubt as to what they want of you, you can always change the scene." But this seems to me like more of the same—another of what my college writing instructors would have called "body paragraphs."

2   The question of how it leaves me feeling is important, I think, perhaps the most important question I can ask about a conclusion. Because if it's the job of the introduction to take me from the title to the body of an essay, then it is the function of conclusions to remove me from the body of the essay, back into the world, with some new sense, feeling, or thought. But it's not just anywhere in the world. I should be delivered, as it were, to a particular place, or at least unleashed in a particular direction.

3   So let's look at the conclusion for Belloc's essay one more time, and consider this: where does he want me to go, what does he want me to do? If my answers to these questions turn up nothing, then I should ask myself, what does he want me to think, or to believe—

what, finally, does he want me to feel:

> And the fifth way is to be Strong, to Dominate and to Lead. To be
> one of the Makers of this world, one of the Builders. To have the more
> Powerful Will. To arouse in all around you by mere Force of Personality
> a feeling that they must Obey. But I do not know how this is done.

4   The tone of this final enumerating paragraph turns suddenly dark and serious, in a way. Or satirical, or perhaps revelatory, when he writes about having the "more Powerful Will," culminating in the notion of obedience. I am left with a sense here, that this essay was not entirely about what it was about. That it has become something else entirely; and that this essay is a kind of commentary on something universal to the experience of getting respect. It leaves me thinking. I find that with a little reflection, the conclusion was here all along—but it was hidden! But the essayist has left me chewing on it; he hasn't spelled it out directly, spoon feeding me like one would a child, but it has become clear enough.

5   I would say that, in response to my original question, that the conclusion and the body of this essay are seamless. That they are so wholly integrated that it seems almost, to one who is not quite paying attention, that there is no conclusion at all. But upon taking a closer look…

The Library

John Pfannkuchen

1   After spending the better part of my life deriding and mourning those who cannot quite seem to keep up with the times, I have found myself backpedaling into the past; I used to preach the gospel of convenience through technology, through cloud computing and the Internet of things; databases and search algorithms.

2   No longer, however. I've since discovered, or rediscovered, the sheer speed and efficiency of strolling into a library and finding five or six books on any subject I'm curious about, and on top of finding the answer I was seeking, learning a host of other things about the matter in the offing.

3   This lesson was taught to me one day when I was having quite the trouble researching an essay with published articles in a scholarly database, since all the relevant articles were behind a pay wall, and everything else was too specific and therefor entirely off topic. I found the sources were nearly useless to answer the questions I had posed to them, except possible by implication—but it would have taken an expert in the subject matter to suss this out.

4   I would spend hours conjuring the best search terminology (which required a specialized knowledge I did not have), combing through search results, trying to determine what was relevant in each twenty page tomb and which wasn't. I'd strain my eyes at the glowing window of a laptop screen or worse yet a smart phone. I figured how convenient! I won't have to leave the comfort of my apartment, or even stand up, to copy and paste my quotations from this or that source! I'll have this essay done in no time.

5   But the first time I walked into a public library it was a revelation. Consider the structure of a book. It begins with a cover, and depicted on this cover is some sort of image, which allows the

average person a quick understanding of what the book is about. This is ingenious! Following this is a title—a good title can convey the heart of a subject; knowing this I can peruse covers quickly— but should I find one that strikes my fancy, just inside the cover is another miracle which one cannot get on the Internet: an index, a directory of chapters, listing major topics, within the book! Running my eyes across this directory tells me whether or not the book is right for my project; no more time wasted scanning dense paragraphs on a screen! Then if I see a particularly relevant chapter, I can just turn to that page and begin reading. If the chapter is not immediately compelling, that's the test of whether or not to take the book.

6 But here's another feature of books—they are portable, and comprehensive, and usually they are both general and specific! One chapter will give a researcher the context they could not glean from hours of essay perusing on a scholarly database.

7 Here's another thing: drive, take the bus, or walk—once there the library is free. I find some librarians to be intimately familiar with the libraries, though your mileage may vary. At my local library the librarian in the reference section has an advanced degree in medieval French history, and knows all the best authors to read. A quick trip to the library and a chat with him had me set up for days of reading and learning in under an hour.

8 So as you can see nowadays I avoid the Internet for formal research. There are several reasons for this. First off, it seems that everyone else is using the Internet, and because of this I fear my work may not stand out among my peers. Another thing is that I find most Internet content incomplete, biased or outdated, plus the amount of scholarly, professional work is limited or very expensive. Additionally, for me at least, using the Internet encourages poor note taking practices. How often do I have to retype, or physically write down, what I find on the Internet? Seldom to never, because I can just copy and paste. I don't even read the whole article, much

less read it carefully. Because of all these reasons I find that writing based on Internet research is difficult and ultimately of an inferior quality. So nowadays I take the easy way out.

9   I tend to read physical books first, and journals articles second. Library journal databases contain mostly academic journal articles. These are published by research universities and independent researchers. Academic journals are important for modern academics, and using them first may seem appealing. But writing may suffer from relying too early on journal articles. Using scholarly journal articles first may force a writer to combine unrelated topics.

10 It's better to begin with a few books. In most nonfiction books there are references to scholarly articles in the back of the book. I would scan the book to get a broad overview of the subject. Then use the references in the back of the book to understand the book better. Then I can search for the articles by author name on an Online research database.

11 Below I have written a short guide for the would be library researcher. If you are interesting in backpedaling into the past with me, continue reading.

12 The first thing to do is to come prepared with your citation page perhaps in a notebook, and a bag to carry your sources (books). Bring some cash or a credit card for the photocopier.

13 Search the (Library) stacks with the Dewey Decimal System. With this handy system you can browse to your heart's content! There's an even more detailed version of the system in an appendix at the

back of this book.

000 – Computer science, information & general works

100 – Philosophy & psychology

200 – Religion

300 – Social sciences

400 – Language

500 – Science

600 – Technology

700 – Arts & recreation

800 – Literature

900 – History & geography

14 Scan each book for relevance first, before checking it out. When you pull each book off the shelf begin with the cover and back. Does it seem relevant to your topic? Now look at the table of contents—that part in the front of the book that tells you all chapters and their page numbers. Look at the Part, Book, Section and Chapter headings. Do any of them jump out to you as especially interesting or relevant to your topic? If so, turn to that place and scan the first page. If it looks useful, take that book. If a book does not seem like it will be useful to you, put it back on the shelf.

15 Now the next part is key: scan the nearby titles on the surrounding shelves. What do you see? Grab any other titles that may be of interest to you. If you find anything interesting, repeat the steps above. Check the Table of Contents and Chapter headings as usual. If there is nothing relevant, then move on. Repeat this process until you think you have what you need or cannot carry any more.

On Quotations

John Pfannkuchen

1   Now, here's another matter that weighs on me in the middle of the night: whether or not to quote directly, or to paraphrase. Have you ever been sitting there, looking at an essay, trying to make a reference to another text, and wondered the same?

2   For me it all boils down to what I'm writing about. I quote when I'm writing about the words themselves (not just their meaning), and I paraphrase when I'm writing about the meaning behind the words (and altering them is easier for the reader than quoting). I choose what to quote the same way that I choose what to paraphrase. I paraphrase if I don't plan on commenting on the way the source is phrased. This way my reference will lose nothing by being put it into my own words. And conversely, I only quote if I plan to comment on the way a source is phrased. I ask myself what exactly the actual phrasing is adding to my essay before including it. If at all possible, I default to paraphrasing.

3   I try to avoid the appearance of having created a patchwork of other's ideas and having branded the result as my own.

4   When writing fiction I paraphrase a character's dialog in the third person like so: John rambled on and on endlessly about the coming of the robot-Dinosaur Apocalypse.

5   Direct dialog in fiction: John cried, "They're coming for us with their long robot necks and their big swishy tails!"

6   A direct quote in an essay is the same as direct dialog in fiction, except I use the surname instead of the given name, and I use a citation: Pfannkuchen writes, "They're coming for us with their long robot necks and their big swishy tails" (1).

7   Notice how the end of sentence punctuation falls outside of the sentence when using a (parenthetical) citation? That is standard

parenthetical citation style--in particular MLA. Another popular style, called APA would look something like this: Pfannkuchen writes, "They're coming for us with their long robot necks and their big swishy tails" (Pfannkuchen, 2018).

8   Also notice how, in all the above examples, it is clear who is speaking, or whose ideas are being expressed? In essay writing I always introduce the work of others to make it clear whose ideas are whose. It should never be vague or difficult to tell if a certain line or idea is either mine, author A's or author B's. The easiest way to affect this clarity is with plain English: "Author writes, 'Quote...'." I prefer the "writes" verb because it is plain and simple, and doesn't distract from the content being discussed.

9   In most cases the first time I quote or paraphrase from a source I try to include some context or background about that source so that my reader understands it's place in the development of my ideas.